OUTLAW TALES
of Wyoming

OUTLAW TALES
of Wyoming

True Stories of the Cowboy State's Most Infamous Crooks, Culprits, and Cutthroats

R. Michael Wilson

TWODOT®

GUILFORD, CONNECTICUT
HELENA, MONTANA
AN IMPRINT OF THE GLOBE PEQUOT PRESS

A · TWODOT® · BOOK

Copyright © 2008 Morris Book Publishing, LLC

Map © Morris Book Publishing, LLC.

Library of Congress Cataloging-in-Publication Data is available on file.
ISBN 978-0-7627-4506-7

Printed in the United States of America
10 9 8 7 6 5 4 3 2 1

To my wife, Ursula

Contents

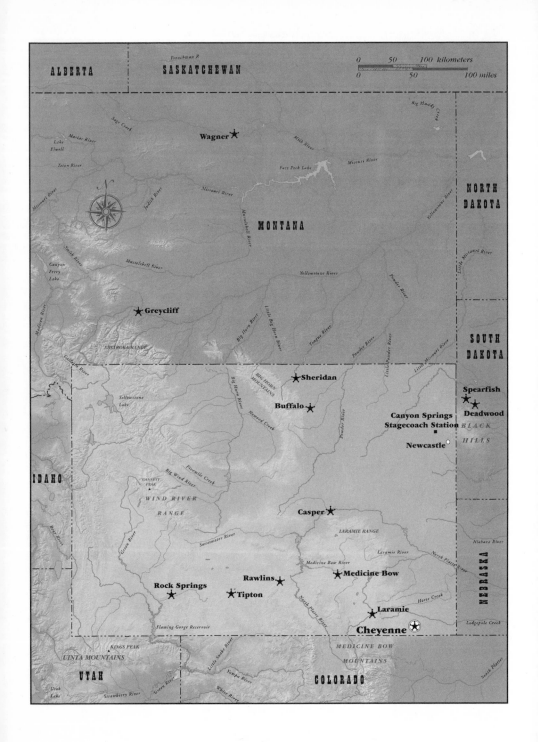

WYOMING

Introduction

In the early days before Wyoming was a state, it was a part of the Dakota Territory. The territory was shaped like a figure eight toppling head first toward the east. It was a region that was overlooked during the rush into Oregon country, and it would not be discovered until the Union Pacific Railroad arrived along its southern border.

On July 4, 1867, Chief Engineer General Grenville Dodge selected a spot near Crow Creek for a terminal and laid out a construction camp for the Union Pacific Railroad. He named the camp and the pass to the west Cheyenne for the Indian tribe living nearby. The first building was raised by July 10. Nine days later, the official survey of the land was completed, and several more buildings were erected. By the end of summer, nearly four hundred establishments were open for business. The population had grown to ten thousand, though many of the residents were transients who worked on the rail line and moved west as the tracks progressed. Still, the city was thriving and had grown at such a phenomenal pace that it earned the title of "the Magic City of the Plains."

Within months tracks had moved farther west to Laramie, and then rapidly continued through the state. Major towns sprang up along the route. From each town, roads branched out north where more settlements were soon established. As population grew, those who would victimize law-abiding citizens flocked into the region searching for opportunities. The tales of those outlaws are an integral part of the history of the territory, which was called Dakota Territory before 1868. On July 25, 1868, the region was separated and became the Wyoming Territory, and on July 10, 1890, it was officially designated the State of Wyoming.

Tracking Wyoming's outlaws through literature is just as difficult, and often as frustrating, as tracking them over a wilderness trail more

Introduction

than a century ago. Everything written about a desperado is suspect, and the most reliable sources for those minute details are the local newspapers of the day. There are those moments as a researcher, however, when you uncover something new about an old story or discover an entirely new tale. Those experiences make the long, tedious hours poring through microfilm worthwhile.

Wyoming before 1900, record reveals, did not have the number of desperadoes found in Texas, the Indian Territories, or in America's Southwest. However, Wyoming did have some of the most flamboyant, bizarre, and desperate outlaws, and had its share of bold and daring crimes, thrilling pursuits and arrests, and spectacular punishments.

Butch Cassidy, his partner the Sundance Kid, and Tom Horn are among the best-known outlaw characters from America's Wild West history; and no criminal record is more bizarre than that of "Big Nose" George Parrott and Frank Towle. In a land of guns, knives, and axes, poison was rarely considered a weapon, yet Wyoming's criminal record supports one such use of strychnine. Among the many "wars" that took place on the frontier, none is better known than the Johnson County War.

Wyoming's outlaws hold a prominent place among the desperadoes of the "wild and wooly West," and they earned it. Presented here are their stories.

Charles Martin and Charles Morgan
Hanged on the Tripod Gallows

Tree limbs, telegraph poles, frameworks for unfinished buildings, barns or stables, balconies or bridges, vigilantes could always find some ready-made gallows from which to hang an outlaw. However, in the earliest days of Wyoming the vigilantes of Cheyenne "built" a gallows to expiate the crimes of two outlaws. Charles Martin and Charles Morgan were hoisted up a tripod gallows only hours apart, becoming the first outlaws hanged in Wyoming.

Cheyenne, the "Magic City of the Plains," was experiencing growing pains in 1867. Because of its isolation, word of the discovery of gold "in the Utah Territory" nearly went unnoticed. The Green River gold mines were two hundred miles from Salt Lake City, which actually placed the gold strike in a remote corner of the Dakota Territory in the middle of what would become Wyoming Territory a year later. But the discovery of gold could not be kept secret for long, and finally reports brought the rush of men to find those mineral riches. As the railroad moved west, the trip to the mines became easier, and several of the towns built at intervals along the railway benefited from the sudden influx of miners and other entrepreneurs.

The Wyoming Territory was not created until July 25, 1868, from parts of the Dakota, Utah, and Idaho Territories. The court system was federal, and so the U.S. district court, and the administration of justice, was suspect in the minds of the populace, who preferred to handle criminal matters locally. An ineffective judicial system usually fostered vigilantism.

Charles Martin had come to Wyoming from a respected family in Lexington, Missouri. As soon as the railroad tracks arrived, he left his home and two children to seek his fortune and settled in Cheyenne.

Cheyenne, Wyoming, in 1868. *Wyoming State Archives Department of State Parks and Cultural Resources*

From the time of his youth, Martin was a desperate character who was a womanizer and drank liquor to excess. He partnered with William A. James, who was known by everyone as Andy Harris, and who was another member of the rowdy element. Together they purchased and jointly managed a dance house. It was rumored that their purchase was financed with stolen money, but there was never enough evidence to prosecute them. They inevitably had a falling out and dissolved their partnership.

The rift that ended their separation began at 5:00 p.m. on February 13, 1868. Martin and Harris met at Thomas & Beauvais Hall on Sixteenth Street. Martin leaned against the bar situated toward the front door; Harris stood five feet from him facing toward the rear of the building.

Harris said loudly, to ensure that everyone present heard him, "You are a dirty little bastard. I ought to kill you. You are no friend of mine; if I did you justice I'd shoot you now." Harris then brandished a Derringer but did not point it at Martin.

Martin put his hand in his pocket and countered, "Shoot! What do I care?"

Harris responded, "No! No! When I shoot you it will be up and up. I'll not shoot you as you tried to shoot me in that stairway. But you're no friend of mine, get out of my house. God damn you, get out of my house or I'll shoot you."

Martin started to back up slowly toward the front door. Suspicious of Harris's next move, he stopped and declared that he would go out the side door instead. Harris held his Derringer above his head. He followed Martin step for step so that five feet still separated the two men when Harris reached the end of the bar. At that point Harris lowered his Derringer, and with that movement Martin pulled a five-shooter from his pocket. Harris fired one shot and missed while Martin fired five shots in rapid succession. Five wounds formed a neat line from Harris's chin to his navel. The wounded man collapsed, and Martin walked calmly out of the side door.

Dr. F. W. Johnson was summoned to the scene, and he attended to Harris, who lingered until 11:00 a.m. the following day, when he died. Dr. Johnson took charge of the body and as county coroner held an inquest. The six-man jury found, "that he [William A. James] came to his death by a pistol shot by the hand of Charles Martin."

After the inquest Martin was arrested on a murder charge and taken before Judge Ara Bartlett for a preliminary examination. Judge Bartlett committed Martin to jail until the next term of the U.S. district court for the second judicial district.

Martin's trial commenced with jury selection on Monday, March 17. Judge Bartlett presided over the trial with District Attorney E. P. Johnson and W. W. Corlett present for the prosecution and J. D. Chord and W. S. Crawford for the defense. The case opened in the afternoon of the following day. Martin's attorneys argued self-defense, and the entire case relied upon the testimony of four eyewitnesses and the attending physician. On Thursday, March 19, the jury of twelve men acquitted Martin on the murder charge. Judge Bartlett, in discharging the prisoner, gave him some sage advice regarding his future conduct and told him in touching words to "remember your mother."

Martin's acquittal created a great deal of dissatisfaction in the community. Had he used common sense and took the judge's advice, Martin would have left town until the matter cooled or at the very least made an effort to remain inconspicuous. Instead, he became more insolent and defiant then ever and began making the rounds of his usual haunts celebrating his liberty and making threats of "furnishing another man for breakfast."

On the Friday evening following his acquittal, Martin went to the Keystone dance house. He joined the large crowd enjoying fiddles and banjoes and danced in the center of the room. According to the *Leader* (Cheyenne), the Keystone was a place "where females of the lowest type may be secured as partners in the dance, while faro tables, keno, and all imaginable games constitute the side dishes."

After midnight a man asked Martin to step outside to join a friend who wanted to see him. As Martin stepped through the door, he was grabbed. The doors were closed behind him and secured from the outside. Immediately, the forty men that were inside drew their pistols and made for the door to see what happened to Martin. Outside they were met by fifteen men in black masks wielding their pistols—men who clearly meant business. The men holstered their weapons when they realized that the masked men were vigilantes. The vigilantes departed with Martin, who was heard to cry out, "My God, men, what are you going to do with me!" The vigilante party disappeared into the darkness dividing into two groups, so that the men following did not know which party had the prisoner. The men hoping to rescue Martin returned to the Keystone empty-handed to await some word of the outcome.

Martin put up quite a struggle but was finally pistol-whipped into semi-consciousness. He was dragged to a spot near the east end of the city where a crude tripod gallows had been erected. A noose tied in a bed cord was placed around Martin's neck and the loose end thrown over the apex of the tripod. The killer of Andy Harris was then drawn up.

The next morning the body was found dangling, the neck and cord stretched so that the feet of the deceased brushed the ground. Martin's limp head had several ghastly wounds from the beating he had received while the vigilantes were trying to subdue him. Two of the town's policemen cut down Martin's remains and delivered them to Coroner Dr. F. W. Johnson. A search of the body revealed a letter from his wife containing a touching appeal for him to forsake his evil ways and return to his family in Missouri. Apparently, the letter was not very persuasive.

Two men were hanged on the same day on tripod gallows.
Eileen Hayes Skibo

That afternoon a coroner's jury was summoned and found: "We the undersigned, summoned as jurors to investigate the cause of Chas. Martin's death, find that he came to his death by strangulation, he having been found hanging by his neck on a rude gallows, at the extreme end of Tenth St., in the suburbs of Cheyenne. Perpetrators unknown."

While the events leading up to the lynching of Martin were unfolding, a span of mules was stolen from W. G. Smith. Cheyenne was only nine months old, but stock thieves already plagued the area around the city. Smith was determined to recover his animals. With the help of the same vigilante group that lynched Charles Martin, Smith made every effort to locate the stolen stock but found no clues. Without any other leads, they seized a man known as "Wild-horse Smith." This Smith, not related to W. G. Smith, was suspected of knowing something about the horse-thief gang, although he was not a member.

Wild-horse was steadfast in his silence, so the vigilantes tied his hands behind him, took him to a tree, and placed a noose around his neck. They gently raised him until his feet hung free and dangled him there until he was unconscious before lowering him. When he regained consciousness they thought he would talk, but he was made of sterner stuff and refused to say anything. He was "pulled up a tree" three more times and each time, when lowered, he gave no clue. When told on the fourth time up that it would be his "last dance on earth," he finally talked. He told of a certain dugout near the creek where stolen stock was hidden.

There were many dugouts on the outskirts of Cheyenne, and most were occupied by honest men, down on their luck but hopeful for some new opportunity. The dugouts were created by digging a small tunnel into the bluff until a habitable-size abode was formed. A small hole was bored upward and lined, and this chimney would allow smoke from a small fire to escape the dugout. No one had thought to look among the dugouts for stolen mules until Wild-horse's lead.

The vigilantes followed their prisoner's directions and found the oversized entrance to a well-hidden dugout. Inside they found fifteen stolen mules and room for more, but W. G. Smith's team was not among them. Armed with this new intelligence, Smith made further inquiries. He learned that Charles J. Morgan, a known member of the horse-thief gang, had "purchased" his four-mule team and some other stock for about half their value. He and a man known only as "Kelly" were driving the stock south on the road to Denver. They were then only a short distance out of town in the mountains. Smith formed a posse, overtook Kelly at Guy Hill, and recovered his mules. Smith's posse captured Kelly, and the party started for Cheyenne. On the way back into town they found Morgan, who claimed that he and Kelly had legally bought the mules and were going to Sweetwater to sell them. Morgan was also captured, and the two prisoners were taken into Cheyenne at an early hour on March 21.

At that time the jail in Cheyenne was little more than a tent over a wooden frame with a wooden floor. A guard manned the flap. So, with escape almost a certainty, and the vigilantes ready for action after recently dispatching Charles Martin, they decided to settle the matter of the horse thieves for themselves.

For the second time that night, the vigilantes constructed a crude gallows tripod by tying the ends of three logs together and then spreading the legs and securing them to the ground. They threw a rope over the apex and put the noose end around Morgan's neck. Morgan was pulled up and the loose end of the rope tied off to one leg of the tripod.

At daybreak the body of Morgan was discovered. His remains had blue and swollen features, tongue and eyes protruding, fists clenched, his feet brushing the ground. A sign pinned to his back announced: this man was hung by the vigilance committee for being one of a gang of horse-thieves.

The U.S. marshal was summoned, and he cut down the body. The coroner's jury preserved the noose for inspection. Morgan's body was taken to the coroner's store and laid out next to Martin, and the same coroner's jury reported:

We the undersigned, summoned by the Coroner to inquire into the cause of death of Chas. or J. Morgan, find the evidence that his death was occasioned by strangulation, he having been found hanging by the neck on three poles in the rear of the Elephant Corral, in Cheyenne, D. T. Perpetrators unknown.

Shortly after Morgan had been hanged, Kelly was taken some distance out onto the prairie. Thereafter, a number of shots were heard. A diligent search was made without result. The search continued until a vigilante leaked information that Kelly had been banished from Cheyenne, and the gunshots were meant to speed him on his way.

The bodies of Martin and Morgan remained on the dusty floor of the back room of the coroner's store until evening. They were then carried out onto the prairie and buried.

The "first" in any endeavor always holds a special place of prominence, and Martin and Morgan, habitual criminals in their individual endeavors, were the first outlaws to be executed in what would become Wyoming. Lynching was outlawed, but it was tolerated—sometimes even encouraged—on the frontier when the law or the courts were not yet established or proved ineffective.

The Asa Moore Gang
Lynched by Vigilantes

When the Union Pacific Railroad left Omaha to lay tracks westward, a makeshift town was assembled at each significant "end-of-track." Each town created by the U.P.'s advance was preceded by another unofficial town consisting of gamblers, saloon keepers, and soiled doves who preyed upon the railroad workers. These unofficial towns often preceded U.P. towns by months, each resident trying to reserve the best location for their operation before the railroad's surveyor arrived to make the town official.

The town of Laramie had been platted by the railroad's chief surveyor, Sam Reed, in February 1867 on land just north of Fort Sanders, which had been established only two years earlier. By the time the first railroad men arrived in Laramie, a tent city had already been set up for two months. Among the first of its three hundred citizens were businessmen planning on establishing legitimate enterprises. The new residents also included the outlaw element, including several men who would become minor players in Asa Moore's gang in Laramie.

The town of Laramie formed a new government on May 1 and the following day elected Melville C. Brown mayor. Brown could do nothing to govern the town because of the rowdy outlaw element, already well entrenched, so the entire slate resigned in three weeks.

As soon as Laramie's elected government collapsed, Asa "Ace" Moore declared himself mayor and appointed O. S. Duggan town marshal. Duggan in turn hired Con Weiger, Edward "Big Ed" Bernard, and "Heartless Ed" Franklin as his deputies. These four men with Moore were known as the "five bosses." To round out the slate, Moore appointed

9

"Long" Steve Young as justice of the peace. Moore was also the proprietor of two saloons in Laramie—the Diana and the Belle of the West. The latter was used as his base of operations for criminal activity.

The five bosses used their authority to recover money from those who won on their gaming tables—not a frequent occurrence. They also arrested other innocent people with money on some false pretext. The five bosses would take them into the back rooms of the Belle of the West saloon, conduct a mock trial, pick them clean, and, if they seemed no threat, turn them loose. If the five sensed trouble from their mark, they would murder him. The bodies of their victims would be buried in unmarked graves on the prairie or dumped in a boxcar to be found later at some distant location.

In August 1868 Duggan, who was embroiled in the controversial shooting of eighteen-year-old Robert Reed, lost his job and was nearly lynched by a mob led by the murdered boy's father. That's when things began to unravel for the Moore gang.

In late September the good citizens of Laramie began organizing a large vigilante committee. The leaders were Tom Sears, an army veteran and legitimate saloon owner; John Wright, a saddle maker; and Nathaniel K. Boswell, a member of the Rocky Mountain Detective Agency. They were determined to rid their town of the unwanted element. They held a people's court with the defendants in absentia, and then planned an organized strike for October 18, 1868, to arrest the guilty parties. The committee had compiled a list of more than fifty undesirable individuals, and among them were six men marked for execution. Moore's gang, the most prominent among the outlaw element in Laramie, was included on the list; and Moore, Weiger, Bernard, and Young dominated the execution list of six desperate men.

At 8:00 p.m. on October 18, 1868, five hundred men gathered on the far side of the tracks behind the railroad repair shops. From there, groups of men deployed to prearranged locations. At the sound of a gunshot fired by Sears, they were to move in and capture their assigned

Asa "Ace" Moore and two gang members lynched at Laramie
Wyoming State Archives Department of State Parks and Cultural Resources

men from the list. Then the plan was to sort them out, hang the six condemned men, and put the rest of the undesirable men and women on a special train out of Laramie—under threat of death should they return.

However, a shot was prematurely fired, unrelated to the plan, and only the party assigned to the Belle of the West saloon was in position. They made their move. The targeted men in the Belle of the West met the attack with gunfire, and the battle lasted fifteen minutes. Con Weiger and Ed Bernard were badly wounded; henchmen Charles Barton, a coronet player, was killed; William Willie, a fireman on Union Pacific's engine 69, was shot through the bowels and expected to die; and William McPherson was shot through the leg but was expected to recover. Many others among the undesirables were wounded, and some may have died later on the train or thereafter.

Weiger and Bernard were taken to an unfinished shed behind the Frontier Hotel, where preparations were made to hang them. Asa Moore, uncertain of his status after the melee, went to the shed and ordered the vigilantes to release Weiger and Bernard. Instead, one of the men stepped up, put his shotgun into Moore's belly, and announced that Moore's name was on the list of six and that he would join Weiger and Bernard. The three men had their hands tied behind them, had nooses placed around their necks, and were hoisted up. It was reported that before they were strangled to death, their bodies were riddled with bullets. The bodies were left hanging throughout the night and well into the next morning.

"Long" Steve Young was captured at Lawson's ranch nine miles from Laramie. He was brought to town and told of the hangings. The committee seemed satisfied that they had hanged enough outlaws for one day, so they ordered Young to leave the city by 7:30 a.m., as he had missed the special train. According to the original plan, he was also ordered not to return to Laramie under threat of death. Stupidly, Young disobeyed his orders and went to the scene of the hangings. When he saw the bodies of his friends still suspended, he declared that "no strangling s__s of b___s" could drive him out of town and challenged any-one to molest him. A half-dozen committee members then stepped out from the crowd and warned him to leave or they would "shoot his brains out on the spot." Young promised that he would leave, but threatened to return with his friends and exact revenge upon the vigilantes. Young, however, reneged on his promise and did not leave town as ordered.

Young was followed around town until 10:00 a.m. and once again was told to leave within the hour, but he again defied and challenged the vigilantes. The vigilantes then seized Young and dragged him to the main railroad crossing at the foot of B Street near the depot, selected a telegraph pole, tied his hands behind his back, put a noose over his head, and pushed him up a ladder. When lynching was imminent Young begged for a chance to leave town, but it was too late. In the presence of hundreds of spectators, without ceremony or delay, the vigilantes pulled the rope taut, tied off the loose end, and jerked the ladder out from under Young's feet. One of the vigilantes thought Young was taking too

"Long" Steve Young was lynched the day after his boss, Moore, was hanged.
Wyoming State Archives Department of State Parks and Cultural Resources

long to die and pulled down on Young's legs, which snapped the rope. Young's body fell. While he lay on the ground senseless, one of his victims rushed forward from the crowd and kicked and stomped his head. The vigilantes pulled the angry man away, tied a new noose around Young's neck, and pulled him up once more. It took but a short time for Young to finish strangling to death.

The committee secured a job wagon and went to the shed to collect the bodies of Moore, Bernard, and Weiger. When Young was declared dead, they cut down his body. The remains of the four men were driven to a place three quarters of a mile from the city and buried in a single wide, deep grave. En route the "women" of the dead men tried several times to pull their man off the wagon, but the vigilantes would not allow it, nor would they allow any kind of marker to be placed over their grave.

Duggan fled from Laramie after he was nearly lynched, and Franklin, who was not on the execution list, was placed on the train and threatened with death if he returned. Moore, Bernard, and Weiger had pushed their luck too far, fleeced too many innocents, and murdered too many good men, but they finally got what they deserved—an ignominious death at the end of a rope. Young, a party to all of Moore's outlaw antics, was given a second chance but failed to heed the warnings, and he joined the others, dangling at the end of a rope from a telegraph pole and then buried in an unmarked grave on the prairie, like so many others he helped put there.

Attack of the Monitor

General Phil Sheridan, Commander of the Division of Missouri, which included Wyoming and the Dakota Territory, wanted a military command within the Black Hills so he could exercise greater control over the Sioux. In July 1874 General George A. Custer was dispatched with one thousand men to make a reconnaissance of the Black Hills. He took along two prospectors. When the prospectors returned to camp on French Creek with a small quantity of "yellow dust," scout Charley Reynolds headed for Laramie, the nearest town with a telegraph, to report the discovery. The rush was on. Within weeks so many men had flocked to the area that the town of Deadwood seemed to spring up overnight. Experienced stagecoach operators John T. Gilmer, Monroe Salisbury, and Mathewson T. Patrick saw the need for transportation and established the Cheyenne and Black Hills Stage and Express Company. On April 5, 1876, their first coach left Cheyenne for Deadwood.

Each stagecoach in the line was named, and the "Monitor" was selected to be a special treasure coach that carried the yellow dust from the gold mines to Cheyenne. Knowing that the Monitor would be a target for stagecoach robbers, Gilmer, Salisbury, and Patrick constructed the coach with state-of-the-art protection. They hired A. D. Butler of Cheyenne to line the body of the Monitor with $\frac{5}{16}$-inch steel plate because it proved to withstand every caliber rifle bullet fired at a range of fifty feet. The roof was the only part not lined, because the heavy metal made the coach top heavy and prone to overturn. The Monitor was equipped with two firing ports on each side of the coach that would allow the messengers to return fire if the coach was attacked. A specially built safe, named "the Salamander," was bolted to the floor and was guaranteed by the manufacturer to withstand a break-in for twenty-four hours.

> ## ROBBERS' ROOST STATION
> ### CHEYENNE AND BLACK HILLS STAGE ROUTE
>
> Along the Cheyenne-Deadwood stage route, stories still are told of outlaws and buried gold. But the swaying Concord stagecoaches stopped rolling in 1887 eleven years after beginning service to the gold regions of the Black Hills in 1876.
> Located at the Cheyenne River crossing, Robbers Roost was a station of the Cheyenne and Black Hills Stage and Express Company. Built in 1877 on a new shortcut, it derived its name from the many robberies in the area. The crossing was the spot most dreaded by stage drivers: steep riverbanks slowed the coaches to a crawl and provided concealment from which lurking road agents could wait the approach of the intended victims.
> Station agent at Robbers' Roost was D. Boone May, also a deputy U. S. marshal and a shotgun messenger for gold-laden treasure coaches from the "Hills." In September 1878, south of here, May and John Zimmerman surprised desperadoes in the act of robbing the southbound coach. The outlaws opened fire and one of them, Frank Towle, was fatally wounded. Outnumbered, May and Zimmerman escorted the coach to safety and the outlaws made their escape. Towle was buried by his companions. May later found the grave, removed Towle's head and took it to Cheyenne in a sack to try to claim a reward.
> The era of the gold rush to the Black Hills was a flamboyant one, bringing together a diverse gathering of frontier characters--Indians, soldiers, miners, stage drivers, tradesmen, housewives, gamblers, prostitutes and outlaws.
> According to legend, Robbers' Roost station was burned by Indians.

The promise of great riches did not draw every man into the Black Hills. Some men preferred to wait along the trail at some isolated spot and "mine" their riches from a treasure box. Almost as soon as the coaches began to operate, the road became infested with road agents. They struck the southbound coaches at night between Robbers' Roost and Hat Creek.

Traveling north from Cheyenne to Deadwood, stops included Hat Creek, Mays Ranch, and Robber's Roost. North of Robbers' Roost the territory became desolate and stops included Jenney's Stockade, Beaver Creek, and the northernmost point, Cañon Spring station, thirty-seven miles south of Deadwood.

During the afternoon of September 26, 1878, the iron-clad Monitor was loaded with three ingots of bullion weighing a total of 546 ounces valued at $17.50 per ounce and 1,056 ounces of gold dust valued at

$13.75 per ounce. The coach also carried jewelry valued at one thousand dollars, half of which was a bag of diamonds, and two thousand dollars in currency. The total value of the treasure on board that day was twenty-seven thousand dollars. The coach was driven by H. E. "Gene" Barnett and carried three shotgun messengers to guard the safe: Gale Hill was on the boot with the driver, and Scott Davis and Eugene Smith rode inside.

The Monitor usually did not carry passengers, but the line had made an exception on this run and carried Hugh O. Campbell, an operator for the Black Hills Telegraph Company, who was planning to disembark at Jenney's Stockade, his new telegraph post.

A lookout in Deadwood hurried ahead of the coach to inform a small band of road agents that there was treasure aboard. The treasure-laden coach had traveled south thirty seven miles from Deadwood to the Cañon Springs stage station.

The station consisted of a stable with small living quarters for one employee. Shortly before the arrival of the treasure coach, a man on horseback rode up to the station and asked for a drink of water. Upon dismounting, he pointed his pistol at stock tender William Miner. The unarmed stock tender had no choice but to comply, and he was locked in the grain room by the road agents. Next, four more road agents joined the group, and they knocked the earth chinking from between the logs of the stable to make gun ports.

The coach pulled to a stop in front of the stable at the Cañon Springs station at 3:00 p.m. Gale Hill called for Miner. When Miner didn't answer, Hill got down from the boot and placed a chock block under the back wheel. He started for the stable. At that moment the robbers opened fire. Hill was wounded in the left arm in the first volley but managed to fire back with the gun in his right hand. He continued to shoot until a rifle bullet hit him in the chest and passed entirely through, knocking him to the ground. Unable to continue fighting Hill crawled to the rear of the stable.

A shot through the roof of the coach ricocheted inside, taking a chunk of wood with it, and both projectiles struck Smith in the forehead, knocking him to the floor senseless. Smith was bleeding profusely from his head wound. Davis thought his fellow messenger was dead or dying and continued to return fire from inside the coach. Eventually, he decided his best course of action would be to exit through the coach door opposite the stable and make his way to a large pine tree across the road. He kept the coach between him and the robbers but continued firing as he backed across the road.

Rather than remain trapped in the coach, Campbell decided to follow Davis's lead. When the telegrapher strayed to the left of the coach, he was wounded and went to his knees in the roadway. All the robbers then opened up on the stationary target, and Campbell, riddled with bullets, fell over dead.

Meanwhile, Davis made it to the tree and continued the gun fight. Coach driver Barnett was still on the boot. Davis called to him, telling him to make a run for it or to take the coach out of the station. However, the wheels had been chocked when they first pulled into the station. Before he could whip-up the six-horse team, road agent Frank McBride ran out and grabbed the leaders. Davis fired at the exposed robber, and McBride threw up his hands, fell over backwards with a stomach wound, and crawled around behind the horses and into the stable. Another robber, Charles Carey, then came out using the coach for cover and ordered Barnett to come down. Carey placed the driver in front of him as cover and then advanced on Davis. The two men exchanged threats, but Davis realized he could not shoot the robber without hitting Barnett and that he needed help. He left the station and started on foot toward Beaver Creek. Davis planned to get help and then return.

Davis walked seven miles to Ben Eager's ranch and borrowed a horse. He soon met messengers Jesse Brown, Billy Sample, and Boone May on the road, who were heading north to investigate the reason the treasure coach had been delayed. The four messengers returned to the station and found the robbers gone, the safe opened, and the treasure captured.

After Davis left, the robbers rounded up all the remaining men and tied them to trees, telling them that someone would be along at 10:00 p.m. to release them. The stock tender freed himself and then the others. Together they headed for Deadwood to report the affair. Hill was taken to the Cold Springs ranch where Dr. F. L. Babcock of Deadwood treated his wounds. At first it was thought he would die, but the arm wound was not serious and the rifle bullet had passed through his body without striking a vital organ, so he fully recovered. Smith's wound proved to be superficial.

The entire countryside was outraged by the robbery. Colonel Adams of the Post Office Department was charged with organizing the Cheyenne posse. He was sworn in as a deputy U.S. marshal, and then selected Scott Davis, Boone May, and eight others for his party, known as the Davis party. They went to Fort Laramie for horses, ammunition, and supplies and then headed north into the Inyan Kara country to pursue the fugitives.

Nearly every day some new party was organized to follow a clue or a trail, each party hoping to collect a portion of the large reward offered by the stage line. The U.S. Government offered two hundred dollars per robber as did the Laramie County's commissioners. On September 28 Luke Vorhees, superintendent of the stage line, issued a proclamation of reward:

> $2,500 reward.
>
> Will be paid for the return of the money and valuables and the capture (upon conviction), of the five men who robbed our coach on the 26th day of September, 1878 at Cañon Springs (Whiskey Gap) Wyo. Ter. of twenty-seven thousand dollars, consisting mostly of gold bullion. Pro rate of the above amount will be paid for the capture of either of the robbers and proportionate part of the property.

After leaving the Cañon Springs stagecoach station, the robbers took separate trails, except for Carey, who remained with the wounded McBride. All five men made their way east into the Dakota Territory. As pre-arranged, they met on Reynold's Prairie at the convergence of the two forks of Castle Creek in Pennington County. The loot was divided, and from there the road agents separated again—Albert Speers headed southeast toward Nebraska; Thomas Jefferson "Duck" Goodale headed east toward his home in Atlantic, Iowa; Carey remained with McBride and they headed east toward Newton's Fork with newcomer Albert Gouch riding point; and the fifth robber was never positively identified.

Carey, McBride, and Gouch arrived at Newton's Fork the following day, where the two robbers traded their saddle horses and two hundred and fifty dollars for two ponies and a spring wagon. Carey threw the saddles in the bed and made the wounded McBride as comfortable as possible. They were seen turning northeast near Rockerville heading in the direction of Rapid City.

Meanwhile W. M. Ward, division superintendent for the stage line, and Uri Gillette were out searching for the outlaws. They cut Carey and McBride's trail at Slate Creek. They followed it long enough to determine that the fugitives were heading toward Rapid City and then hurried ahead to gather a posse. Ward learned that the spring wagon had been seen the evening of September 27 near Rockerville and would probably be at Rapid Creek the following day. The posse quickly moved down Rapid Valley, but was unable to find the fugitives' tracks. The robbers had slowed their progress because of McBride's wound.

At dusk the posse camped near Mitchell Creek, and one member reconnoitered the surrounding country. He discovered the fugitives' camp well hidden in a small ravine near Pine Springs a short distance off the road. The horses had been turned out to graze, and three men were well settled. Believing he had not been observed, the man returned to the posse's camp. The men discussed the situation, and Ward decided they would make their attack upon the robbers' camp at daylight. As dawn broke the posse surrounded the camp and found that "the birds had flown" leaving behind the wagon and a few supplies. The posse could find no tracks, but knew from their trail that the fugitives had relentlessly pursued an easterly course. Ward, alone, went east to Pierre expecting to intercept the robbers there or at least find some clue.

Gouch separated from the robbers and went to Fort Thompson while Carey and McBride decided to head west, turning back into country they knew well. They rode throughout the early morning hours and were well away from their camp by daybreak on September 30. They continued riding until they were back inside Wyoming. By October 2 they had made their way to Jenney's Stockade, traveling only fifty miles in thirty-six hours. Near the Stockade the two fugitives ran headlong into the Davis party. Having seen him holding the leaders at the stagecoach station, Davis knew McBride on sight, and recognized the wound he had inflicted upon the robber. Carey was recognized as the man who had used Barnett as a shield.

21

On October 3 a stage driver confirmed to the *Deadwood Times* "the hanging of a road agent near Cañon Springs and says others will soon share the same fate." On October 9 Cheyenne's *Daily Leader* reprinted a story from the *Deadwood Times* as follows:

The Good Work Progresses. Deputy Sheriff's Davis [not Scott Davis] and Radcliff of Central, returned yesterday and reported that they found the bodies of two men hanging to a pine tree about seven miles from Jenney's Stockade, at a point four miles east of the road from the stockade to Custer. They were black in the face, with tongues and eyes protruding, and were a ghastly looking spectacle. Both wore the California riveted brown clothing and had light colored hair and moustache. They had been hanging for some time, and it is thought that the Scott Davis party did the good work last week. The sheriffs did not molest them, but left them to swing and fester in the sun, a warning to others of the same ilk.

None of the men in the Davis party ever confirmed that they hanged these two men or that those hanged were Carey and McBride. However, the *Leader* provided a description of the two fugitives, which coincided with the description of the two hanged men.

Two of the Cañon Springs stage robbers are described as follows: Charles Cary [*sic*], 27 years old, light complexion, brown hair; if any beard, little sandy; six feet high; has new, large Ulster overcoat, a little gray; carries a Winchester cartridge belt; pockmarks on each side of his nose. . . . Frank McBride, who is supposed to be with Cary [*sic*], is a small man, with small features; small feet, light brown hair, light moustache and goatee; weighs 145 pounds; is 24 years old; very sharp eyes, supposed to be wounded.

Meanwhile, stage line superintendent Ward went to Pierre expecting to find some word of Carey and McBride, but instead got a lead on Thomas Jefferson "Duck" Goodale of Atlantic, Iowa. He went to

Goodale's hometown and saw on display in a bank's window the stolen gold bar marked "#12" worth $4,300. He inquired within and from bank owner Almond Goodale learned that Almond's son had received the bullion as payment for a rich mining claim in Wyoming. Ward had "Duck" Goodale arrested, and his father turned over the gold and other stolen items to authorities.

On his way to Wyoming for trial, Goodale escaped from the train by going into the washroom and slipping out of his shackles. The bands and chains were found on the floor, but Goodale was gone. The *Leader* reported:

> Duck Goodale, the road agent who escaped from Ward at Lone Tree, Neb. on Tuesday night, is thus described in the circular issued by the stage company: About twenty seven years old, five feet eleven, and weighs about one hundred and eighty pounds; has dark hair and when he escaped wore a thin beard of two week's growth.

The stage line offered a reward of seven hundred dollars for his capture and Laramie County added two hundred dollars, but he was not heard of again.

Albert Speers sold eight hundred dollars in gold dust and five hundred dollars in jewelry in Ogallala, Nebraska. A detective became suspicious and arrested Speers at Wood River as he was trying to sell more jewelry. Speers was returned to Wyoming and convicted of second-degree murder on November 28, 1878. He insisted that he had arrived late at Reynold's Prairie and received a short count on his share, which seems likely since he was found with less than two thousand dollars. Speers was sent to the penitentiary in Nebraska to serve his time. His sentence was commuted on April 26, 1886, and he received a full pardon, restoring all his civil rights, on September 24, 1889. In all he served only ten years and ten months for his part in the robbery and for killing Campbell.

Andy Gouch was apprehended but not prosecuted, since he was not present at the robbery and murder. Perhaps the decision not to prosecute him was a deal that later lead authorities to hidden gold dust valued at eleven thousand dollars—perhaps the recovered amounts from Carey's and McBride's shares.

The attack on the Deadwood stage was one of the best planned robberies—and worst planned escapes—in the history of Wyoming. Of the twenty-seven thousand dollars stolen, approximately three fourths was recovered. The amount missing corresponded to the share for one man, and it was thought by most that the infamous "Big Nose" George Parrott was that fifth man. Parrott would pay the ultimate penalty several years later for a murder unrelated to the robbery at the Cañon Springs stage station. All the other robbers but one were accounted for—proving that, for most outlaws, crime does not pay.

"Big Nose" George Parrott and His Boys

It was always news when a "badman bit the dust." In Wyoming in the early 1880s three badmen died, but it was the manner of their deaths and all that followed that made the headlines. One fugitive was shot to death and then beheaded, another was "pulled up a telegraph pole" and left dangling, and the third was hanged and then skinned.

"Big Nose" George Parrott led a gang of criminal miscreants in the late 1870s that engaged in robbery, rustling, and murder. They were the most active Wyoming criminals of that period. When they tried to wreck a train for robbery—the first attempt in the West—an alert crew prevented the derailing. The criminals killed two lawmen in the process. Outlaws Parrott, "Dutch Charley" Bates, and Frank Towle eluded arrest for several years before their careers ended.

It all began on August 19, 1878. Parrott, whose real name was George Francis Warden but was best known as "Big Nose" George, assembled his men for an assault on Union Pacific's westbound express No. 3 train near Medicine Bow, Wyoming. Parrott's gang consisted of Charles "Dutch Charley" Bates, Jack Campbell, Joe Minuse, Tom Reed, Frank Towle, Sim Wann, and John Wells. The eight men loosened a rail near Medicine Bow to wreck the train. Train assaults and robberies had been covered in great detail in the newspapers of the day, so Parrott knew how to go about wrecking the first western train for the purpose of robbery.

An alert section foreman, however, discovered the loosened rail. He warned the engineer and the authorities, and then repaired the rail before the next train passed. The Parrott gang, seeing their plan foiled

This photo of George Parrott was taken in Omaha, Nebraska, prior to his extradition.
Wyoming State Archives Department of State Parks and Cultural Resources

and knowing a posse would soon be on their trail, fled toward Elk Mountain. They found a hiding place in Rattlesnake Canyon among the cedars, where they waited to ambush the posse. Soon Deputy Sheriff Robert Widdowfield and Special Union Pacific Agent Tip Vincent came within rifle range of the robbers. As soon as the lawmen were in their sights, Bates opened fire on Widdowfield and killed him instantly, while Parrott took careful aim at Vincent killing him instantly.

Needing food, supplies, and money to make their escape, the gang next robbed the Trabing Mercantile on Crazy Woman Creek. They stole the supplies they needed, and Parrott, who liked his liquor, also stole two barrels of whiskey and a horse to pack it on.

The gang fled north into Montana and laid low for some time among a group of unsuspecting trappers on the Musselshell. Desperate for transportation, Parrott arranged to trade some of the stolen whiskey to Indians for stolen horses. The gang drove the horses north and sold them in Canada. Next they stole a herd north of the border and drove them south and sold them at Fort Benton.

In early December 1878 a man from Fort Benton visited the town of Rawlins and told of a big-nosed man named George Reynolds who had been bragging around town of his exploits. Several of Rawlins's best men were immediately dispatched to Fort Benton, but Parrott was already gone. The men interviewed the townsfolk and listened carefully to the stories Parrott had told them. Among the stories were the details of how the Parrott gang planned to derail the No. 3 train, and how Bates had killed Widdowfield and Parrott had killed Vincent.

Bates's description was circulated, and he was arrested at the Pioneer Hotel in Green River by Albany County Deputy Sheriff John LaFever. He was lodged in the jail at Laramie City. After a short stay at Laramie City, Bates was being taken to Rawlins for trial, but the prisoner got no further than Carbon City.

On January 5, 1879, passenger train No. 3—the same train the Parrott gang planned to wreck in August 1878—stopped in Carbon City at

9:25 p.m. A party of masked men boarded the train, overpowered officer Ed Kern, and took his prisoner—Dutch Charley Bates. Without ceremony or delay they marched Bates to a telegraph pole adjacent to the station and threw a rope over a crossbar. The noose end was fastened about Bates's neck and then the only delay was when they allowed him to confess to the killing of Widdowfield. Bates begged them to shoot him to death rather than hang him, but he was hoisted up and allowed to slowly strangle. The entire affair was handled with such efficiency that the train was only delayed thirteen minutes.

Meanwhile, Frank Towle was still on the run. He had been with the Joel Collins gang in Deadwood, but when that ill-fated gang of stagecoach robbers went south into Nebraska to rob a train, he decided to stay behind and continue to rob stagecoaches. Towle joined the Parrott gang, and on September 13, 1879, Towle with John Irwin and several others from the Parrott gang stopped a northbound stagecoach four miles south of Lance Creek in Sweetwater County. They took the mail and the express box before ordering the driver to continue on. When the southbound coach arrived at the same spot, Towle stepped into the road, fired his gun, and ordered the driver to halt. Boone May, reputed to be the fastest gun in the territory, and John Zimmerman were riding as messengers. When they heard the shot, May returned the gun fire with a single shot killing Towle. A gunfight then continued for thirty minutes, but the messengers could not dislodge the other robbers so the southbound coach finally continued on its way. The following day a posse went to the scene and searched, but the body of the dead road agent could not be found, and many doubted that May had killed his man.

Three months later John Irwin was arrested for the Lance Creek stagecoach robbery and he told May where the body of Towle had been buried. May hurried to the scene and dug up the grave and, finding the body badly decomposed, severed Towle's head and buried the rest of his remains. He put the head in a box and carried his gruesome prize to Cheyenne in Laramie County to collect the two hundred dollar reward, but the head was too decomposed to identify and no reward was paid. May then took Towle's head to Carbon County to collect a reward posted there, but again he was unable to collect the reward. When the rotting head became too offensive, he disposed of it.

Meanwhile, Parrott was still on the run, and he and his boys pulled off several successful stage holdups. The reward for Parrott's capture had grown to two thousand dollars. He had no choice but to hide out. However, as his funds dwindled and his courage increased, he surfaced again along the stage route between Miles City, Montana, and Deadwood, Dakota Territory. Fully masked and using scatter guns similar to those carried by Wells, Fargo & Company messengers, Parrott and his boys succeeded in a particularly lucrative stagecoach robbery in July 1880.

Parrott obtained so much loot during that robbery that he decided to retire for a while. However, Parrott was recognized by the landlady of a Miles City, Montana, boardinghouse, who was on the coach that day. Parrott was busy spending his ill-gotten loot in a Miles City saloon and bragging, as usual. Meanwhile, the landlady was turning him in to the authorities. Word soon reached Rawlins, and within hours Sheriff Robert Rankin and a deputy were on their way to Miles City. Parrott was arrested without a struggle and taken by train toward Rawlins for trial.

In Carbon City on August 7, 1880, twenty masked men boarded the train and took the prisoner from the lawmen. They took him onto the station platform, put a noose around his neck, and yanked him up. They then lowered him and asked for a full confession. When the prisoner hesitated, the men pulled him up several times and then promised that if he talked he would stand trial, but if he did not confess he would be left hanging with the loose end tied off. Parrott talked, and once he began he gave every detail of his various criminal ventures, some of which were quite a surprise to the vigilantes. The mob, true to their word, then returned the prisoner to the custody of Sheriff Rankin.

Parrott was tried at the fall 1880 term of the district court in Rawlins, found guilty of the murder of Tip Vincent. On December 15 the defendant was sentenced to hang on April 2, 1881. The condemned man seemed to sit quietly in his cell awaiting his end, but all the while he was planning an escape.

On March 20, 1881, he made his move. At 7:30 p.m. Sheriff Rankin entered the jail corridor to lock down the prisoners. Parrott had managed to remove his heavy, homemade-iron shackles. He used them as a weapon, striking Rankin on the head numerous times. The blows knocked the lawman semiconscious and inflicted several serious cuts. The sheriff's wife, who resided in the jailhouse building, heard the scuffling and rushed into the jail where she locked the door to the cells, her husband still inside with the prisoners. She then got a revolver and stood guard while her sister ran downtown to sound the alarm. A force of men immediately came to Sheriff Rankin's rescue, and Parrott was locked in his cell. Extra guards were then placed in the jail, more to protect the prisoner from potential lynch mobs than to prevent an escape.

Sheriff Rankin knew that a lynch mob was being organized and asked the townsmen to wait the short time remaining before the prisoner was to be legally hanged. However, the general opinion was that the sheriff had taken enough abuse from the prisoner, and that Parrott might attempt another escape if left to await his fate on April 2.

On March 22 at 10:55 p.m. a party of thirty masked men went to the jail and took Parrott from the jail. They marched him to a telegraph pole in front of the Hugus & Company store on Main Street. A rope was placed over the crossbeam of a telegraph pole, the noose around the prisoner's neck, and Parrott was stood upon a barrel. Parrott begged piteously to be shot and cried out that it was mean to hang him, but his pleas were ignored. When the barrel was kicked out, his feet did not clear the ground, so he was taken down. A ladder was brought, and he was coaxed and pushed up the ladder to an acceptable height, and the noose was again placed around his neck. His last words were a plea, "I will jump off, boys, and break my neck," but the ladder was slowly pulled away. Without a sudden drop, he dangled for some time before he slowly strangled to death.

After hanging for a day, Parrott's body was cut down by Coroner A. G. Edgerton, who took the remains to Daley's Undertaking Parlor. Assisted by Dr. John E. Osborne, Edgerton conducted an autopsy. After the examination was complete, Dr. Osborne made a plaster of paris death mask, cut a large skin sample from the chest area, and kept the skull cap, which had been removed to examine the brain. Autopsies were not uncommon in the Old West, but it was unheard of that parts of a corpse were retained as souvenirs.

The rest of the remains were then turned over to the citizens of Rawlins, who were not yet done with vengeance upon Parrott. They placed his remains in a whiskey barrel filled with a saline solution. The barrel and Parrott's pickled body were buried in an unmarked grave without ceremony. Later Dr. Osborne tanned the skin sample and sent

Artist's conception of the lynching of "Big Nose" George Parrott; original altered to conform historically. *Eileen Hayes Skibo*

the human leather to a shoemaker, requesting that each shoe be made so that one of Parrott's nipples was placed at the tip of each shoe. The skinning had not been done properly for that purpose, so when the shoes arrived there were no nipples on the toes as requested. Nonetheless, the doctor still wore the shoes on special occasions. The skull cap was given to Osborne's assistant, Dr. Lillian Heath, and used as a doorstop.

In 1950 the barrel was dug up during a construction project, and the contents proved to be human remains. After some curiosity and confusion, the remains were identified as Parrott's by fitting the skull cap, which was still in the possession of Dr. Heath, to the remainder of the skull. The skull cap and the shoes made of human skin are now on display at the Carbon County Museum in Rawlins.

The Parrott gang was among the worst in Wyoming's outlaw history: stealing horses; murdering innocent men for robbery; trying to wreck a train, which could have resulted in great loss of life; and murdering two popular lawmen from ambush. Most of the men in Parrott's gang paid a penalty for their lawlessness, but none were more gruesome than the deaths of the main characters and the treatment of their remains.

Henry Mosier and His Dog Tip
On a Crime Spree

Outlaws, those habitual criminals who seemingly could not help but commit crimes, usually started out with petty offenses and often fled to new locations during their criminal career to avoid an arrest, which would interrupt their criminality. These offenses often escalated until, for those outlaws of prominence, they committed one of the more heinous crimes of the Old West.

The most serious of crimes was, of course, cold-blooded, premeditated, first-degree murder. So it was with Henry Mosier. His crimes escalated from fraud and wife beating to the attempted murders of two men and the brutal murder of another man for the purpose of robbery. He began his criminal career in the Dakota Territory, at least as far as the record shows, but he was a bad man and may have had a long career of petty violations not worth documentation. However, his worst crimes, and his ignominious death as a result, were in Wyoming. His only true love and concern, it seems, was for his dog Tip.

Henry Mosier came west during the early years of the Wild West. By 1883 he was familiar with the territory between Deadwood and Cheyenne, and this would later help him elude the lawmen on his trail. Mosier married one of the Halliday sisters (her first name is unknown), and the couple settled in Deadwood. In August 1883 the Mosiers had a falling out and separated. Mrs. Mosier hired Deadwood attorney Lorring F. Gaffey to recover from her husband one span of horses and two colts that belonged to her and that Henry had taken without permission. Henry compromised the case by falsifying a mortgage on the horses supposedly to secure a payment of a note. The attorney found that Mosier did not own any horses and the mortgage was a fraud. He confronted Mosier and threatened further legal action. Caught red-handed, Henry then went to the home of his wife and, according to Gaffey, "beat her in a shameful manner."

Mosier immediately left the country on foot with his black Newfoundland dog named Tip and a companion who had a good pony. When the men were 10 miles from Deadwood, Mosier shot his companion, whom he left for dead, and took his pony. Mosier and Tip headed south. Miraculously, the wounded man crawled to Deadwood, swore out a warrant against Mosier for assault with intent to kill, and fully recovered from his wounds.

Mosier left Dakota Territory for Longmont, Colorado. About September 1, 1883, he hitched a ride with a freighter and traveled into Wyoming. At Hat Creek, Mosier met freighter James Knight and hitched another ride, this time toward Cheyenne. Knight had an outfit of eight mules, a covered freight wagon, and a trail wagon coupled behind the larger wagon. At Fort Laramie the two men were joined by twenty-five-

Mosier stopped at Hat Creek Station while fleeing from South Dakota.
Wyoming State Archives Department of State Parks and Cultural Resources

year-old John H. Wensel. Wensel had been working on the government farm near Fort Laramie. He was on his way to Nebraska to file a claim on some land. Mistakenly, Wensel mentioned to his traveling companions that he was carrying money in his satchel. At that moment Mosier hatched a plan. He decided to steal the money and Knight's outfit.

That night the party camped six hundred yards east of Fort Russell. All three men slept in the freight wagon—Knight at the front, Wensel in the rear, and Mosier in the middle. Mosier was the restless sort and usually woke early, so nothing seemed peculiar the following morning when he arose before the others. Except instead of his usual morning routine, Mosier put his plan in motion. He got the ax and struck Knight on the head with the blunt end.

Seeing that his first victim was senseless, he hurried to attack Wensel, striking him on the head. This time the blow only awakened his second victim. Mosier struck Wensel again, but the young man fought back. The two grappled for the ax while Wensel kicked at Knight trying to awaken him, but the old man made no more than a grunt. Wensel wrestled the ax from Mosier and threw it out of the wagon. Both men jumped to the ground, and Mosier ran to a locker at the forward end of the wagon. He took out a pistol and ordered Wensel to give up his money.

Wensel asked, "Do you mean to rob me?"

Mosier replied, "It don't matter, give up your money."

Wensel said, "I'll give it up, only don't shoot."

Wensel then tried to climb into the wagon from the rear when Mosier shot him. The ball passed entirely through his body tearing out part of his liver and passing through the bottom part of both lungs. Wensel fell and, despite his injuries, crawled under the wagon, out the other side, and then got up and ran toward the nearby fort. Mosier pursued his victim and fired three more shots—one being so close that when Wensel threw up his hands to protect himself, the ball shot off part of his left thumb.

Oliver Gordon, a member of the Ninth Infantry stationed at the fort, had set out to do some duck hunting early that morning when he heard the shots. He saw the two men running toward him. Mosier saw Gordon, armed with a shotgun, coming toward them, so he gave up his pursuit of Wensel and ran over the hills toward Dry Creek and out of sight. Gordon considered chasing Mosier, but Wensel cried out, "For God's sake, come and help me!"

Gordon responded and supported the wounded man as they started for the fort hospital, but soon Wensel collapsed. Gordon went into the fort and got the hospital attendant and a stretcher. They returned to Wensel and carried him to the hospital, where they summoned post surgeon Dr. Richard S. Vickery. The doctor dressed the wounds, five in number, and reported that at least two were of fatal proportion. Wensel was still awake and gave a full statement of the crime and a description of the murderer, whom he identified as H. Moore. When it was clear he was dying, Wensel endorsed his statement as his ante-mortem declaration. Wensel died on September 13, 1883, and at 5:00 p.m. was buried in a corner of the city cemetery. His fortune of $53.10, which Mosier never secured, spared him from an unmarked grave in potter's field.

While Wensel was dying, the pursuit posse found Knight. He was taken to Cheyenne and cared for. While there, he gave his statement implicating Mosier as the person responsible for the attack. Meanwhile, Mosier fled over the hill to where Knight's mules were hobbled. He selected the gray and rode it bareback to Thomas Cahill's, Mosier's brother-in-law (at this point Cahill was not yet officially divorced), arriving just an hour after the incident. He asked to borrow a saddle, but Cahill, who wanted nothing to do with his good-for-nothing soon to be ex-brother-in-law, refused to give him one. Mosier rode away.

An hour later the wife of Constable Ben Smalley noticed the gray mule at the stable in back of their house. She recognized it as one that her husband had previously sold to Knight. It was later supposed that Mosier had left the mule there and walked, where he either caught a wild horse or continued on foot. By September 13 all eight of Knight's mules were accounted for: the gray in town, another near Camp Carlin, and

the other six mules still hobbled on the prairie where they had bee̶
to graze.

Mosier was a wanted man. Rewards of one hundred dollars were
posted by Sheriff Seth K. Sharpless and by County Commissioner
Thomas Swan for the capture of Mosier. Governor William Hale also
issued a proclamation bringing the total reward to seven hundred dollars. The proclamation stated:

$500 REWARD

Governor's Office,

Territory of Wyoming,

Executive Department,

Cheyenne, September 13, 1883

It appearing to me, upon the request of the prosecuting attorney, of
Laramie county, territory of Wyoming, that H. Moore, *alias* Henry
Mosier, had committed a felony within said county and territory,
namely the crime of murder, and that he has not been arrested, in pur-
suance of the authority vested in me by law, I hereby offer a reward of
five hundred dollars, the same being the amount recommended by said
prosecuting attorney for the arrest and delivery into the custody of the
sheriff of the said county, of the said accused, who is described in the
application made to me by the said prosecuting attorney, in the following manner: "Moore is described as a man of about 40 years of age,
medium height, weight about 175 pounds, hair of a color between light
and dark, head partially bald, sloping forehead, chin whiskers and mus-
tache of same color as his hair. When last seen he wore a black slouch
hat, dark coat, dark woolen shirt, with a row of buttons in front, dark
pants covered with blue overalls and boots."

I also order the printing of 300 postal cards containing a copy of
this reward. All of which expense and reward will be paid out of the

county treasury of said county, upon my certificate that the same has been earned.

Done at the executive office in the city of Cheyenne on the 13th day of September, A.D. 1883.

Wm. Hale,
Governor of Wyoming

The postal cards were widely distributed throughout the region, one coming into the possession of Sheriff John Sweeney of Larimer County, Colorado. Sweeney decided to pursue the fugitive when he was contacted by Jim Cliff, a ranchman living near Laporte on the Old Laramie and Denver Trail. Cliff provided information to Sweeney about the fugitive's whereabouts. After identifying Mosier's trail as the seldom used Old Salt Lake Trail, Sweeney turned over the pursuit to his brother Peter, whom he deputized for the task. Peter Sweeney followed the trail. Soon the fugitive and his dog, Tip, came into view. Deputy Sweeney caught up with Mosier and asked him how far it was to Louisville, the next town on the trail. While Mosier replied that he did not know, the lawman got the drop on him. When Deputy Sweeney took the coat from Mosier's arm, which the murderer had been clutching, he found inside a .45 caliber Colt revolver with a fifteen-inch barrel, one chamber empty, four containing expended cartridges, and only one cylinder loaded. Tip snarled at Sweeney as he put the handcuffs on Mosier, but the dog did not attack. The fugitive and dog were placed in the buggy and taken to Louisville before continuing on to Fort Collins.

Word was sent to Cheyenne, but this was the second "certain arrest of Mosier," and every effort had been taken to prevent a lynching when the first suspect was brought to Cheyenne. It was good work on the part of lawmen because the first man was not Mosier and therefore innocent of the crime. Now, to be certain, a special train was dispatched to Fort

Collins at 10:45 p.m. carrying Sheriff Sharpless, two deputies, and a citizen's committee. They were anxious to determine if they had the right man, as they would not call off the search until certain, and several hundred men were out searching every gully and ravine around Cheyenne. The train reached Fort Collins after 3:00 a.m., and Sheriff Sharpless wired Cheyenne: "Fort Collins, September 16, 1883; 2:45 a.m. – Have Mosier; no mistake. Start back at 2:45 Cheyenne time. Greeley."

At 3:10 a.m. Sheriff Sweeney, his brother Peter, and a deputy U.S. marshal met the train accompanied by the party of citizens, and in a short time the prisoner and his dog were brought to the depot. Mosier and Tip were surrounded by reporters. Mosier addressed the crowd.

> I think I am arrested for killing two men. I don't know if they are dead or not; don't know if I know Knight or Wensel, may know them by sight. I was going to Leadville. I came from Cheyenne; started Wednesday night. I stayed in a house near the electric light house. I have been in Cheyenne a month. I know Curtiss, know Tom Cahill; I am Cahill's brother-in-law. I rode a gray mule Wednesday morning to Cahill's and asked for a saddle, and left the mule near the lake. My name is Mosier, was born in Ogdenburg, N.Y. in 1839. I am acquainted in Deadwood; my wife lives there. I was at Hat Creek, but rode some with two or three outfits. I camped with Curtiss once at the electric light house. My dog's name is Tip. A man on the road told me about the murder.

He asked several times if the men were dead, and when asked, "Mosier, why did you murder those men?" he denied any knowledge of the crime.

The train arrived in Cheyenne at 6:00 a.m. and lynching was feared, but the large crowd allowed the officers to take their prisoner to the jail. During the day small groups of men gathered and discussed the situation, but there seemed no organization to the gatherings. By 9:00 p.m., however, the many groups seemed to be coming together and an effigy of a man was hanged at Eddy and Eighteenth Streets.

By midnight the mob had organized, and soon afterwards a large body of masked men armed with shotguns and revolvers charged down Nineteenth Street firing their weapons into the air. Every effort had been made to get Sheriff Sharpless to vacate the jail, but he remained in the cell with the prisoner. The leaders entered the jail and overpowered the guards, but Judge Joseph W. Fisher refused to raise his hands and wrested an iron bar from one of the lynchers. The judge was restrained and the bar taken back, and this was later used to pry open the jail doors. The men battered and pried at the jail doors causing considerable damage before they opened the right cell and found Mosier cowering in the corner.

Two men entered and grabbed the prisoner by his ears and pulled him from the cell, where as many hands as could reach him grabbed on and pulled him out into the street, where the rest of the mob awaited his arrival. At various points, as the opportunity presented itself, one of the lynchers would strike out at the murderer, and one blow left him somewhat senseless. The crowd became boisterous when they saw Mosier, and several men fired their guns into the air.

They hurried along with their prisoner to Nineteenth and Eddy Streets where a convenient telegraph pole was selected. A noose was placed around the prisoner's neck and the loose end passed over a crossbeam. At that moment Secretary Elliot S. N. Morgan rushed into the midst of the mob and made an impassioned appeal to spare their victim, not only from mercy, but from justice and a regard for their own feelings. The crowd hesitated in their efforts, in order to listen, but the plea was to no avail. Mayor Joseph M. Carey next tried to reason with the mob, but he had no more success than Morgan.

While the two men tried to convince the mob of five hundred men to abandon their plans, Mosier stood with head down betraying no emotion. He seemed in a semi-comatose condition but recovered sufficiently, just before he was swung off the ground, to call for his dog. Twice he was pulled up and then lowered, and each time when he regained consciousness his only concern was for his dog Tip. When he was pulled up the third time, the loose end was tied off and he hung until life was pronounced extinct.

The work was accomplished by inexperienced hands, as Mosier was battered severely by the protruding iron steps of the telegraph pole. The body was cut down and taken in charge by County Coroner John T. Chaffin. He summoned a jury consisting of H. E. Bauchuer, James Knight, Harry Blake, J. W. Jones, O. P. Goodwin, and C. W. Stewart. Twelve witnesses were examined, and the *Leader* noted, "The amount of ignorance exhibited by the witnesses before the coroner's jury has been something astonishing." Mosier was found to have been strangled to death by persons unknown. He was buried in an unmarked grave in potter's field that evening.

Outlaws typically committed a series of similar but unrelated crimes, like a series of stagecoach, train, or bank robberies. The *crime spree*, however, seems more a modern innovation, but that is exactly the sort of adventure Henry Mosier embarked upon. He began with minor offenses, but quickly escalated from the brutal beating of his wife to an attempted murder of his companion as he moved from one territory into another. He concluded his spree with a most brutal killing and another attempted homicide. He probably would have killed again and again to avoid arrest, without hesitation or remorse, if he had been given the opportunity.

George Cooke

He Had His Man for Thanksgiving

Mary Ann Cooke (sometimes spelled Cook) gave birth to son George in Worcestershire, England, on October 18, 1854. Four years later her husband died, and Mary Ann spent the next eighteen years raising her seven children—four boys and three girls. One son, upon reaching adulthood, found employment in the East Indies, but the remaining six children immigrated to America with their mother in 1876. The family settled in Laramie, Wyoming.

George's brother Albert and sister Mary Ann, named for her mother, settled in Laramie while his brother James moved to Rock Creek. One sister moved to Fort Russell and the other sister moved to Denver, Colorado. In 1883 Mary Ann married James Blount, a large, forty-year-old man who spent a good deal of his time in the many saloons of Laramie. He worked as a janitor at a public school building, but relied upon his wife for a substantial portion of their income. They had a son they named Samuel, and on November 25, 1883, Mary Ann gave birth to a second child, a daughter.

George, who had little education, first found work as a cowpuncher at various ranches near town. Later he found more permanent employment as an ostler and coal-heaver with the Union Pacific Railroad at their Medicine Bow roundhouse. George was considered a good worker, but it was obvious that he had a wild streak.

On the evening of Wednesday, November 28, 1883, George hopped a freight train from Medicine Bow to Laramie. His purpose was to see his new niece and spend Thanksgiving with his family. The train arrived before daybreak. It was too early to disturb his family, so Cooke, who

Dapper George Cooke as he appeared before his execution.
Eileen Hayes Skibo

had developed a fondness for liquor while a cowpuncher, went to a nearby saloon for a few beers. From there he moved on to another saloon and had several drinks while waiting for the gunsmith to open his shop, then picked up the .45 caliber six-shooter he had left for repair during a previous visit to town. George continued his rounds of the saloons and by mid-morning had crossed paths with his brother-in-law and brother Albert. The three men continued their drinking at one place after another with no further thought of family or Thanksgiving dinner.

George was an inoffensive man when not indulging but became rude and contentious when under the influence of liquor. His brother-in-law Blount was always a bully, but especially so when he was drunk. During the course of the day, Blount threatened several times to pummel George, who had never hidden his displeasure at his sister's choice of a mate. George threatened to kill Blount if he tried.

The three men parted company about noon, before any trouble developed, with George and Blount continuing their sprees in separate saloons while Albert went his own way. After nearly a dozen hours of hard drinking, George was ready to initiate, rather than fend off, trouble. He went to the railroad's oil room and robbed the workers of their loose change, then went to another saloon to spend his windfall.

At 6:30 p.m. George was in Cleveland's Saloon, where he announced that he would kill Blount the next time he saw him. A half hour later he was in J. Fred Hesse's Saloon on Front Street. He left the saloon with two men to eat dinner. George stepped onto Front Street and nearly collided with Blount, who was coming out of Abrams' Saloon two doors away. George loudly insulted and threatened Blount, who tried his best to calm the situation and offered to buy George a drink, but finally threatened to beat George if he continued his harangue. Without warning or further provocation, George drew his pistol and pointed it at Blount's head, then fired a single shot. The ball entered Blount's left cheek just below his eye, the blast burning and blackening the skin around the wound. The ball ranged through Blount's brain and lodged against the back of his skull. He died instantly.

George fled west on Front Street, threatening pedestrians as he went, and vanished into the darkness. A posse was organized and went out in every direction in search of the murderer. After 8:00 p.m. George was seen near the rolling mills at the foot of North B Street. There he went inside and tried to sleep, but he was too restless and had moved on before he could be arrested. He made his way to the railroad tracks and threw away his pistol, which was later found by the city marshal during the night. At 7:30 a.m. George was found skulking around the railroad tracks trying to find a boxcar in which to hide.

He was arrested by Harry Smith, a railroad worker, and Cooke said that if he could have made it to Medicine Bow he would have gotten a horse, never to be seen again. He was lodged in an eight-by-ten-foot cage in the Albany County jail.

On December 1, 1883, an inquest was held, and George Cooke was charged with murder. On December 3 he was indicted, and four days later his trial commenced. He did not deny the killing, but said he could remember nothing. As his defense he stated that he was too intoxicated to have formed "malice aforethought" or to premeditate the murder, as required for a finding of murder in the first degree. Nevertheless, the jury found him guilty of first-degree murder, and within a few days Justice Jacob B. Blair sentenced him to hang.

An appeal followed, which delayed the execution, and during that period George spent his time in jail singing, telling obscene stories, and reading every newspaper and periodical he could obtain. During the early days of his confinement he made one feeble attempt to escape, but then settled in to await the outcome of his appeal. The supreme court spent nearly a year considering the request for a new trial before upholding the lower court's decision to deny one. The date of George's execution was then scheduled for December 12, 1884. An application for commutation of sentence to life in prison was submitted and just as quickly denied.

George's mother, infirm and unable to bear up, returned to England. Three days before his execution George wrote to Blount's widow, his sister Mary Ann, to ask her forgiveness. At first she refused but then reconsidered and forgave him. However, she would not visit him.

The night before his execution George spent time conversing with his deathwatch guard William Tatham before retiring after 11:00 p.m. He slept soundly even though a bright light burned in his cell all night. Upon arising he made his toilet and then dressed in his burial clothes— a white collarless shirt, blue suit pants, and new shoes, but set aside his suit jacket. He ate a hearty breakfast and then received Reverend Father Hugh Cummiskey, who heard his confession and blessed him. After the priest left, the doors of the jail were flung open and more than two hundred curious people filed through to have their last look at the condemned man and bid him farewell.

George was described as five foot ten, one hundred and sixty pounds, with sandy hair and a light sandy beard he had grown since being incarcerated. His time in jail had left him pale, but he had gained a little weight during the previous year. The doors to the jail were closed when Father Cummiskey returned at 10:00 a.m., and the priest spent those last hours with Cooke.

A temporary board structure had been attached to the rear of the courthouse building to house the gallows and obstruct public view of the execution. At 11:00 a.m. Sheriff Louis Miller called together the five reporters and escorted them into the execution building. A photographer was already in place with his camera set up. The priest, wearing a cassock and stole, led the procession to the scaffold a few minutes later, with the prisoner at his side. Sheriff Miller and Deputy James Sterling followed closely behind, and then came the jurors and witnesses walking two by two. In all, fifty men assembled within the execution building.

Father Cummiskey continued his prayers for two minutes after the condemned man was upon the trap. The prisoner had taken his position facing the scaffold. The priest turned him to face the crowd, took his hand

and said, "Good-bye, George," and the prisoner responded in kind.

As soon as the priest left the platform, the sheriff stepped forward and asked, "George Cooke, have you anything to say why the sentence of the law should not be passed upon you?" George replied, "Nothing." The prisoner's hands were tied behind his back with a piece of rope, one strap was tightly bound about his chest to hold his arms, another was buckled just below his hips to secure his wrists, and a third strap was secured about his ankles. The sheriff produced a black velvet bag. The rope was put over Cooke's head, cinched and positioned, and the black bag was pulled over his head. Both lawmen stepped back, and at 11:20 a.m. the supporting post was jerked out and the trap was sprung.

City physician Dr. J. H. Finfrock, and Drs. Newell K. Foster, P. F. Guenster, and Lewis S. Barnes monitored Cooke's pulse. Just before the drop his pulse was at two hundred beats per minute; at one minute after it was eighteen; at two minutes thirty-two; at three forty; at four twenty-five; at five eighteen; at six sixteen; at seven and eight fifteen; at nine ten; and at ten minutes after the drop George Cooke's heart ceased to beat. He was pronounced dead.

The coroner's jury of six men was summoned, and they delivered a verdict in accordance with the circumstances. The body hung a total of fifteen minutes before being cut down and placed in its coffin. Examination of the body revealed that the deceased's neck had been broken in the fall, but he never lost his grip on the crucifix in his right hand. The black bag was removed, and Cooke appeared more asleep than dead, except for a deep red contusion about his neck. The lid was fastened on the coffin and just after noon he was buried in the city cemetery at the county's expense.

And this is where George Cooke's story ends. He participated in activities of robbery and murder with no remorse. A cold-blooded killer, Cooke chose to become an outlaw. Perhaps most characteristic of how bad to the bone this outlaw was is that he perpetrated his worst crimes on Thanksgiving Day, a day set aside for peaceful family gatherings.

Benjamin F. "Big Ben" Carter
The Badman from Bitter Creek

Benjamin F. "Big Ben" Carter was born in Texas in 1850. He was a substantially larger than average man in stature for those times. Measuring over six feet tall and weighing more than two hundred pounds, Carter had broad shoulders, balding blond hair, and piercing blue eyes. Because of his dominant size, or perhaps in spite of it, he was a bully, seldom missing an opportunity to upbraid a man smaller than himself. When sober he was surly and vile, but when under the influence of liquor he turned into the worst sort of brute, physically abusing anyone unable to stand against him. He called himself the "Badman from Bitter Creek" and made a concerted effort to live up to that sobriquet.

Carter arrived in Wyoming in 1877 and soon became known as one of the best cowpunchers in the territory. In the early 1880s he was promoted to "top-hand" for the Charles Herbertz Land and Cattle Company. In 1886 Carter gained employment with the Hub and Spoke ranch. Although Carter was a good employee, he spent his idle time getting into trouble. His worst and final offense, the murder of a defenseless boy, was a senseless act and typical of the sort of behavior expected from the Badman from Bitter Creek.

On October 4, 1886, Carter and a group of Hub and Spoke Ranch employees left in the company's wagon for Sweetwater to attend the town's roundup. On the way Carter separated from the crew and stopped at Jim Averell's road ranch, where he drank an ample supply of whiskey before catching up with his fellow employees at their campsite thirty miles from Rawlins. Among the group was James Jefferies, a small quiet boy of seventeen years who had only been with the outfit for two weeks. As soon

Ben Carter, the "Badman from Bitter Creek" the day of his execution.
Eileen Hayes Skibo

as Carter arrived, he singled out the teenager for abuse and threats, and warned the boy to be gone by morning. Carter accused the boy of spying on the outfit, pulled his pistol and, while he had the drop on the youngster, kicked and slapped the boy several times. A short time later he repeated the abuse. No one intervened to help him, so Jefferies turned into his bedroll for the night to avoid further abuse by Carter.

The rest of the outfit, facing an early start, soon joined Jefferies in the tent and rolled into their blankets for the night. Carter joined the men in the tent and rolled into his blankets as well, but soon he began shooting at the tent's roof. (Although speculative, he later claimed that someone told him to.) One of the shots, however, was not aimed at the tent, but rather in the direction of the boy, who lay on the ground a short distance away. The bullet took effect in Jefferies's head above the left eye, passing entirely through. Carter arose and, without waiting to see how badly he had injured his last target, dressed quickly, saddled a good mount, and fled. The boy never awoke and died in nine hours.

Two Hub and Spoke cowboys, who were in the tent when the killing took place, rode to the camp of their foreman, a short distance away. The foreman sent the riders along to warn the other ranchers in the area that Carter might try to swap for a fresh mount from their string. The riders went to the Hub and Spoke Ranch and told Tom Sun, one of the owners, of the murder. Carter arrived at the ranch soon after the riders departed, looking for a fresh mount, so Sun disarmed him and sent him into Rawlins under escort. The party arrived at 8:00 p.m., and the prisoner was turned over to a deputy sheriff and lodged in jail.

The following morning, October 6, Carbon County Coroner George W. Durant summoned a jury for an inquest and found the killing to be a "willful, malicious and unlawful murder." Durant, also a justice, conducted the preliminary hearing a week later. Carter could not hire an attorney so one was appointed, and his counsel immediately, and successfully, filed a motion for a continuance until the May 1887 session of the district court. At the trial, which lasted only one day, testimony concluded by mid-afternoon of May 21, but arguments lasted until 9:00 p.m. The jury then deliberated until midnight before returning a guilty verdict on the charge of first-degree murder.

Carter was sentenced to hang on July 8, but the defendant was now supported by his family and had acquired excellent counsel, so the appeal that was filed stayed the execution. The state's supreme court finally upheld the lower court's decision, and the date of execution was rescheduled for August. However, Governor Thomas Moonlight intervened and granted a respite of sixty-three days so he could consider the prisoner's application for a new trial. The application was denied by the state's supreme court, so Carter's counsel next applied for a reversal of the judgment based upon an error in jury selection, but this was also denied. In July 1887, with all hope lost for a legal remedy, Carter attempted to escape with the aid of a jail trusty, who had smuggled in a saw blade and six-shooter for the prisoner. However, the escape items were discovered before they could be used, and thereafter Carter was chained to the iron latticework of his cell.

During Carter's final days Reverend R. E. G. Huntington baptized him, and on the Sunday before his execution he took communion in his cell. Deputy L. C. Kelley was assigned day and night as Carter's death-watch, and he had to put up with a great deal of abuse from his prisoner. Carter had become despondent, ate little, and seldom slept, so there was some concern that he might try to cheat the hangman, but he only laughed at the idea. On Carter's final night, however, he seemed to brace-up and ate a hearty supper. He received a reporter and told the newsman that he was ready and had attended to his affairs.

After the jail closed for the night, Carter sat with his forehead resting on his hands. He smoked continuously, read from his prayer book occasionally, and once sang a few lines of "Nearer My God to Thee." He slept only two hours. When he arose he ate a hearty breakfast before Reverend Huntington joined him at 8:40 a.m. for an hour of spiritual encouragement. Just before 10:00 a.m. two dozen friends were admitted to bid him farewell and, as soon as they left, County Physician Dr. T. Getty Ricketts and Sheriff William High appeared and informed the condemned man that he would begin his walk to the scaffold in ten minutes. Carter was given a shot of whiskey to calm his nerves, and then the prisoner asked that the hanging be delayed one hour. The sheriff said he would grant this final request.

It was the weather, rather than the 18-foot board fence, that kept most of the curious from attending the execution. However, a crowd of about one hundred spectators arrived despite the weather. At 10:30 a.m., a half hour sooner than agreed, Sheriff High entered the jail with several deputies and brought Carter from his cell. The procession proceeded through the sheriff's living quarters to the scaffold with Reverend Huntington following the prisoner and guards, the sheriff leading the way.

The scaffold had been built against the east wall of the courthouse so that the party stepped through an open second-story window directly onto the platform. Carter took his position on the trapdoor, and deputy Thomas Hanks applied the straps that pinioned his arms and legs. The prisoner thanked the sheriff for his treatment while in jail and then noticed the attending physicians, Drs. Ricketts and John Osborne, and bid them farewell.

The noose of ⅝-inch hemp was heavily lubricated with soap. It was cinched tight and carefully positioned by Deputy Kelley, who also pulled the black silk cap over Carter's head. At 10:37 a.m. Sheriff High cut the cord that held the trap. The trapdoor fell and Carter dropped four feet, breaking his neck. In only four minutes the doctors pronounced life extinct. The body was cut down, placed on a board, and carried into the jail. Those who had braved the cold were rewarded with one final look at the murderer, and were awarded a small souvenir of a piece of the hanging rope. Carter had asked Reverend Huntington to take charge of his body. The reverend delivered a simple burial service that afternoon and then deposited Carter's remains in a grave in the Rawlins Cemetery.

Carter was a heartless, thoughtless bully who murdered a young boy out of pure meanness. The boy not only had done him no wrong, but had made every effort to avoid a confrontation. Typical of the bully, he fled after his cowardly act and when captured denied any responsibility for the killing. He had spent years violating the "code of the West," always on the edge of outlawry, until he finally committed a crime so heinous that he forfeited his life as a consequence.

The WSGA Lynching at Spring Creek Gulch

Sometimes, in the Old West, it was difficult to determine who was an outlaw and who wasn't. The Wyoming Stock Grower's Association (WSGA) was organized in April 1872 to protect the interests of the territory's livestock producers, which amounted to two dozen cattle barons who lived in the east or abroad. For nearly two decades the WSGA had used every means to protect their "rights," including the hiring of "cattle" or "range" detectives, a term for men who were not much more than hired guns or outright assassins.

During those early days WSGA cattle and range detectives protected the open range by murdering men "suspected of rustling." Later, they were hired to prevent homesteading of the range, which the cattle barons claimed by the precept of prior use, even though they were at odds with federal law. This effort finally spread to the battle for the range between sheep and cattle owners. For over five decades many innocent men and one woman were killed to preserve the WSGA's interests. Among the most outrageous acts was the lynching of a man and a woman for no other reason than to regain control over a mile of water rights along a creek.

John and Sarah Ann Averell gave birth to a son they named James on March 29, 1851, in Horton, Renfrow County, Ontario, Canada. The Averell family moved to upstate New York while James was an infant, but both parents soon died and an older sister in Wisconsin raised him. James Averell quit school at sixteen and took a job trailing Indians and recovering stolen stock, but after four years he tired of that work and

Jim Averell as a young man. *Wyoming State Archives Department of State Parks and Cultural Resources*

enlisted in the army. He was first assigned to Company H, Thirteenth Infantry and ordered to Fort Douglas just northeast of Salt Lake City in the Utah Territory. His next billet was Fort Steele on the west bank of the North Platte near Rawlins, Wyoming. His duties required him to guard the Union Pacific Railroad tracks, but again he spent part of his time pursuing Indians to recover stolen stock, which required him to see a great deal of that part of Wyoming.

Averell fell in love with the region and was determined to settle there when he finished his tour of duty, but when he was discharged in 1876 he quickly re-enlisted and was assigned to Company D of the Ninth Infantry. While on assignment at Fort McKinney near Buffalo, Wyoming, he got into a number of verbal disputes with other soldiers and officers but came through with little more than a court martial, fine, and demotion. Now disillusioned with military life, Averell decided it was time to move on. When his enlistment ended in June 1881, he declined re-enlistment and was honorably discharged.

Averell returned to Fort Steele and took a job with the sutler, a man selling provisions to the army. While there, he filed for a homestead on Cherry Creek in Sweetwater Valley north of Rawlins. In 1881 he spent the Christmas holidays with his family in Wisconsin, where he met Sophia M. Jaeger.

Averell married Sophia on February 23, 1882, and took his bride back to their home in Wyoming. By the time they reached the Sweetwater Valley, Sophia was pregnant with a son. In August complications arose, and both Sophia and the premature infant died.

Averell put his heart and soul, and every waking hour, into his work over the next three years, but his homestead held too many bad memories. In July 1885 he filed a new homestead claim fifteen miles to the north, between Horse Creek and Sweetwater River in Carbon County, and he abandoned the old homestead. He built two log buildings on his new claim, one to serve as his home and the other a road ranch consisting of a small store, a saloon, and a restaurant. Averell was appointed postmaster

Ellen "Ella" Watson was characterized as a terror on horseback, who dressed as a man. *Wyoming State Archives Department of State Parks and Cultural Resources*

on June 29, 1886 and later he was also appointed a justice of the peace and notary public, but four months earlier he had met the new love of his life.

In February 1886 Averell met Ellen "Ella" Watson, who was working at the Rawlins House as a cook and domestic. Both being Canadians, they hit it off immediately. Averell offered Watson a job as cook at his road ranch and she accepted. By May a relationship had developed between the two, and they traveled to Lander in Fremont County to file for a marriage license. However, they were never married, likely because marriage would have clouded title to additional land Watson wanted to homestead.

Averell encouraged Watson to file on a piece of land under the Homestead Act (see endnote) and she filed on one hundred and sixty acres adjacent to his plot, giving the couple control of over three hundred and twenty acres of prime range real estate. Watson moved onto her land and began to make a variety of improvements, including construction of a cabin and a corral—a requirement of the Homestead Act to "prove-up" on the land in five years.

The couple's adjacent lots were right in the heart of the open range, and ownership was perceived as an obstruction to the large cattlemen, especially to Albert John Bothwell, who was a prominent member of the Wyoming Stock Grower's Association and had a nearby ranch. Averell and Watson had gained control of more than a mile of riverfront on Horse Creek near where it emptied into the Sweetwater River, and Bothwell was determined to have the land and water rights "restored" to him. The cattle baron tried to buy out the couple. When they refused to sell, Bothwell threatened them. Still they would not give up their right to homestead their claims.

Instead, Watson filed for a permit to dig irrigation ditches and used her savings from her cook's pay to buy twenty-eight unbranded cattle from John Crowder at Independence Rock in the fall of 1888. In December she filed for registration of a brand but the Carbon County Brand Committee refused her application, so Watson bought the "LU" brand from John Crowder. This brand had first been filed by Eugene Shara on November

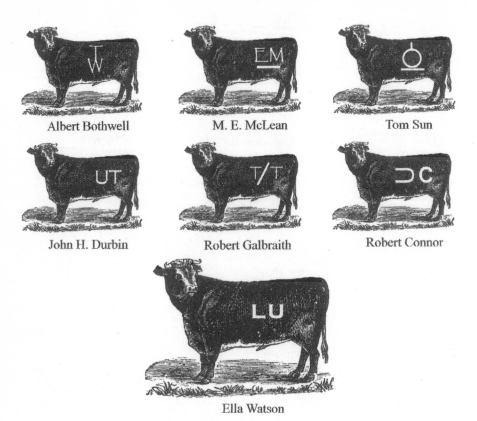

Albert Bothwell M. E. McLean Tom Sun

John H. Durbin Robert Galbraith Robert Connor

Ella Watson

Ranchers claimed Watson and Averell were rustling cattle, but the brands could not be altered to an "LU."

15, 1880, and transferred to Crowder on December 8, 1886. The brand was transferred to Ella Watson on March 2, 1889, and the bill of sale was documented in Record B, page 169 by B. S. Ross, County Clerk for Carbon County. She placed her bill of sale for the cattle and the papers pertaining to her brand in a safe deposit box in a Cheyenne bank. Watson was so anxious to obtain her own brand it is a certainty that her cattle were immediately branded with the LU irons that Crowder gave her upon sales of the brand.

With Watson and Averell moving inexorably toward proving-up on their land, Bothwell became desperate and realized he had to act quickly. He sent George R. Henderson, a cattle detective working for John Clay, with specific instructions to examine Watson's small herd and report back to the authorities that the cattle were stolen, regardless of what he found. Cattle detectives did whatever they were told by their employers, so the thought of making a false allegation or committing perjury was of little concern to Henderson. Following orders, Henderson went to the ranch and returned on the morning of July 20, 1889, to report that Watson's cattle had been rustled, and then he hurriedly left for Cheyenne so that he could not be questioned further on the matter; but Henderson also had another mission in Cheyenne.

Armed with the formal accusation made by Henderson, six prominent members of the WSGA, including Bothwell, who owned the TW and Broken Box ranches; M. E. McLean of the EM Bar ranch; Tom Sun of the Hub and Spoke ranch; John H. Durbin of the UT ranch; Robert M. Galbraith of the T bar T ranch; and Robert B. Connor of the Lazy UC ranch, started for Watson's homestead. When they arrived Durbin tore down Watson's fence and drove her cattle out onto the open range. The men next hitched up her team, went into the house and dragged Watson out, then forced her to drive her buggy as they directed her along. Two local boys were at the Watson ranch when Ella was abducted: fourteen-year-old John L. DeCorey and eleven-year-old Gene Crowder. DeCorey tried to follow but was warned off with a pistol and threats of death. The six cattlemen escorted Watson to Averell's road ranch and forced him, at gunpoint, to join his fiancée in the buggy. Meanwhile, DeCorey and Crowder followed at a safe distance and reported the circumstances to the cowboys at Averell's ranch.

Frank Buchanan, a close friend of the kidnapped couple, followed the trail and found the couple standing in the shallows of the Sweetwater River, their hands tied behind their backs. Buchanan hid and watched, afraid to take action with his friends under the guns of the cattlemen. The kidnapers threatened to drown Averell, but Watson laughed and said that the river was so shallow at that place that they probably could not manage the task. The six cattlemen then escorted their prisoners to the point where the river turned into Spring Creek Gulch, Buchanan following under cover, and roughly pulled the couple out of the buggy. They placed a noose around Averell's neck, forced him to stand upon a large boulder, threw the loose end of the rope over the stout branch of a cottonwood tree, took up the slack, and tied off the loose end of the rope. They next did the same for Watson, which was done with some difficulty as she struggled to keep the noose off her neck. However, she could not fight off six men so finally she stood next to Averell, the noose taut.

Buchanan, to this point, believed that the actions of the men were only intended to scare his friends, and the behavior of the pair showed that was also their belief, but now it appeared that the six men really meant to hang the couple. Buchanan, doing all he was able, fired his rifle at the kidnapers, but they returned a withering fusillade and he had to duck into a hiding place. When he was able to look out again he saw the men push Averell off the boulder and, in but a moment, Watson followed her fiancé. Buchanan could do nothing with six armed men guarding the pair as they slowly strangled to death, so he returned to Averell's ranch and reported the lynching.

As soon as Buchanan saddled a fresh horse he started for Casper to summon the sheriff, but when he had traveled twenty five miles to homesteader Tex Healy's shack he and his horse were spent, so Healy went on to report the affair. The following morning Healy reached Casper and notified Deputy Sheriff Philip Watson (not related to Ella). The deputy gathered a posse and started for Averell's road ranch early Monday morning, July 22 and arrived by late evening. Buchanan had returned to the ranch to await the lawmen, and he immediately joined the posse and guided them into Spring Creek Gulch, where they found, by lantern light, the decomposing bodies of the couple still hanging from the tree limb.

The bodies were cut down and later buried southeast of Averell's road ranch with an oak wagon wheel marking each grave. At the inquest on July 23, convened by acting coroner B. F. Emery, a seven-man jury heard an abundance of testimony, including the positive identification of the six men responsible for the hanging. They found that the deceased died by hanging, but found little more evidence of use in a prosecution.

Henderson, who had hurried on to Cheyenne, had already begun a campaign to vilify the dead couple. The two major newspapers in Cheyenne, the *Sun* and the *Daily Leader*, were controlled by the large cattle barons, and soon Averell and Watson were characterized as two of the most desperate criminals to ever live in Wyoming. According to these publications, "Honest men went in constant fear of their lives," and Averell was identified as the head of a gang of cattle rustlers and was credited with several murders. Cheyenne's *Sun* reported of Watson: "The woman was as desperate as a man, a daredevil in the saddle, handy with a six-shooter and as adept with the lariat and branding iron . . . a holy terror who rode straddle, always had a vicious bronco for a mount and never seemed tired of dashing across the range."

Watson was said to be a prostitute who plied her trade at Averell's road ranch. She reportedly accepted stolen cattle as payment for her favors and consequently had acquired the sobriquet "Cattle Kate" in Douglas. Allegedly, she went by the alias Kate Maxwell and had robbed a faro dealer; poisoned her husband, and "shot a black boy who stole her diamonds." However, the Kate Maxwell described was another person, but the identity and exploits of the real Maxwell, and many more fictions, were superimposed upon the life of Ellen Watson in an effort to further besmirch her reputation.

As time passed more publications took up the stories of Cheyenne's newspapers and embellished on the theme of Averell and Watson as desperate characters. Cheyenne's newspapers were so successful in their campaign to slur the good names of the deceased that none of the six men were ever arrested, and three in particular—Bothwell, Durbin, and Sun—were characterized as "shining citizens" who had performed a great service for the residents of Sweetwater Valley.

The Wyoming Stock Grower's Association would later organize an army to invade Johnson County, where they murdered two men before being surrounded by a superior force. They hired Tom Horn, who would murder several "rustlers" settled on land claimed to be open range, but Horn paid the ultimate price—his life—for a murder he probably did not commit.

In later years the WSGA had thousands of sheep shot or clubbed to death, and they murdered a half-dozen men who owned or tended them. With the exception of the lynching of Averell and Watson, the leaders of the WSGA did not dirty their hands, but it was their money and influence that ended the lives of so many innocents. Their outlawry is a stain on the history of Wyoming.

Endnote: The Homestead Act, passed in 1862, gave millions of Americans the opportunity to own land by granting them title at no cost. A homestead required a house and the 160 acres surrounding it, which was the amount of land deemed necessary for a family farm. Any citizen, or person promising to become a citizen, could file a claim, but the person had to live on the land, farm it, and make other improvements for the claim to "prove-up" in five years. Those eligible had to be twenty-one years of age and the head of a household, or have served in the Union Army during the Civil War. A "head of household" could be a widow, abandoned woman, or an unmarried woman; and "service in the Union Army" meant that boys as young as eight in 1862, who may have served as drummers or buglers during the Civil War, could qualify as well. The Homestead Act encouraged settlement of the frontier, and over 270 million acres were settled in thirty states by this enactment. The law continued until 1986, with Alaska being the last state to benefit from this federal law.

George A. Black

A "Black Day" for Ol' Tanglefoot

George A. Black was born in Indiana in 1862. When but a boy he moved with his parents and five siblings to Ryan County, Missouri. After his father died, the family moved to Davis County. He was a sickly child unable to attend school. When he turned eighteen years old he left home for Laramie, Wyoming. There his health improved and he married a fifty-three-year-old widow with several children. The marriage lasted only four years, and after that Black moved onto a small piece of land not far from Laramie, located next to the far superior claim of Robert Burnett.

Robert Burnett, who was known as "Ol' Tanglefoot," had lived near Meridian, Missouri, during the Civil War, where he lost everything, including his wife. After the war he started westward, settling at several places for a while. After a decade of wandering, he finally settled in Wyoming. Though quite peculiar he was a likeable sort. His friends described him as an "eccentric." He wore gunnysacks, tied with wire, on his feet. He ate only with his hands and threw the scraps on the floor of his cabin, and had not been known to bathe in many years.

Burnett was feeble-minded and terribly superstitious, but he was also a litigious old man. Burnett sued his neighbor, George A. Black, for harvesting the old man's hay. Burnett won the suit, and when Black could not pay the judgment, the plaintiff was awarded Black's buildings, some hay land, and a few cows. With no place to live, and the better part of his poor land gone, Black had no choice but to vacate his property.

Black wanted Burnett's land and held a grudge when he lost his property. He tried to drive the old man off the land and played upon Burnett's superstitious nature by posting White Cap notices—crude

George Black as he appeared while awaiting his appointment with the hangman.
Eileen Hayes Skibo

drawings of skulls, crossbones, and coffins—on his cabin door. Once, he hid in a clump of sagebrush and fired on Burnett, but missed his mark. The old man, instead of turning and running, charged and captured Black. Black insisted that he had mistaken Burnett for an elk, so the old man released him without charges being filed.

When Black failed to drive Burnett off the property, he moved to Medicine Bow, but soon returned to the Pole Mountain area near Laramie to live with his brother Benjamin. There Black found a willing accomplice to help him in his ongoing battles with Burnett. Black first met twenty-eight-year-old Dwight "Roxy" Rockwell at the JD Ranch in Wyoming's Silver Crown mining district. Black and Rockwell became reacquainted in Laramie, where Black explained how Burnett had "stolen" his land. Rockwell agreed to go with Black to Burnett's land to help him reclaim "his" property. Black filed a mining claim on Burnett's property in Laramie, and then the two men stocked their wagon with supplies and started out.

They arrived at Burnett's cabin on May 28, 1889, and found the old man seated on an overturned pail cutting seed potatoes inside his cabin. Rockwell stood nearby while Black talked with Burnett. Black asserted that the land belonged to him and asked, then commanded, that Burnett vacate the property, but the old man refused. Suddenly Black pulled his six-shooter and shot Burnett in the back. When Burnett reached for his rifle, Black shot him in the head and then fired one more ball into the dead body.

The two men wrapped the head and then the entire body of Burnett, hauled it up a remote canyon, and placed it at the end of a huge log. They piled pitch pine onto Burnett's remains and set it afire before returning to the cabin to sleep. In the morning they scrubbed the wagon and smeared grease on the tarp to cover the bloodstains before returning to the body. They raked what remained of Burnett into a pile and, with a new pile of tinder, again set it afire. Then they returned to the cabin and replaced the blood-stained floorboards. That night they returned to Burnett's remains, gathered up the larger bones and remnants, and buried them in a gopher hole. Black and Rockwell took possession of the cabin, but Rockwell soon left for North Park, Colorado.

Burnett was not missed for several weeks. When friends finally noticed his absence, Black explained that the old man had sold out to him and gone east to spend his final days with his daughter. That story was soon discredited, but there was no evidence of foul play, so no action could be taken. There was talk of organizing a search, but this was abandoned when Black threatened to kill any organizer of an investigative committee.

The Pullman family, Charles, Mattie, and teenage daughter Mary, had recently arrived from Missouri. On August 6, 1889, Mattie and Mary were berry picking when they saw a strange pile of ashes covering an area nearly 8 feet in diameter, certainly no campfire. They investigated and found small human bones, bits of wire, and small remnants of clothing. They hurried home and told Charles. The next day the three returned to the site. Charles Pullman examined the remains, gathered every bit of evidence he could find into two pails, and carried them to Laramie.

Pullman gave the pails to the Albany County attorney, who called in Dr. John W. Harris. The doctor and his associate identified the remains as human finger bones, part of a skull, teeth, and a rib bone. They also found rivets from overalls (like those always worn by Burnett), hobnails, and bits of baling wire. Coroner Dr. J. H. Hayford convened a jury and over five days of testimony and investigation found the remains to be Burnett's. The Black brothers and Rockwell were charged with the murder.

George Black and his brother Benjamin were arrested and jailed. At the preliminary hearing before Justice Charles E. Carpenter on August 22, George was held and Benjamin was released. The evidence against

Black, though circumstantial, was very strong. Two weeks after the discovery of Burnett's remains, Sheriff Charles Yund learned that a check payable to Burnett had been endorsed by Rockwell and cashed in North Park, Colorado. Yund deputized J. J. Moore, and the two men went in search of the fugitive. Rockwell was working in a field on George Fletcher's ranch when the two officers found and arrested him. He willingly returned to Wyoming and confessed all the details, first to officers and then under oath at Black's trial.

In mid-October Black was indicted for first-degree murder while Rockwell was indicted as an accessory after-the-fact. The trial in the district court commenced on Saturday, November 2. Five days later Black was found guilty. On November 16 Judge M. C. Saufley sentenced Black to hang on January 15, 1890.

Rockwell was tried after Black and received a light sentence, in consideration of turning state's evidence, and two years later was living in Montana. The appeals process, financed by his brother Benjamin, began for Black. The execution was stayed while the state's supreme court considered the matter, but the respite was only six weeks in duration. The supreme court denied the bill of exemption and upheld the lower court's decision. Governor Francis E. Warren quickly denied the petition for commutation of sentence, and the date for Black's execution was rescheduled for February 26, 1890.

Black had been a Baptist, but a week before the hanging he was baptized into the Catholic faith. On Tuesday evening, February 25, the prisoner was talking with his deathwatch guards when the reporter from the *Leader* was escorted to his cell by the sheriff. In the cell were papers and books read to him by the guards, a bouquet of flowers, and a potted plant. The reporter offered to print whatever the condemned man wanted to disclose and encouraged him to confess, but he professed his innocence and persisted in saying Rockwell committed the crime and that he was denied a fair trial. Just before the visitor left at 9:50 p.m., Black ordered his last breakfast of fried chicken.

Mr *James Stirling, Ex Sheriff*

You are hereby invited to be present at the execution of

GEORGE A. BLACK,

which will take place at the Court House, in Laramie, Wyoming Territory, on the 26th day of February, 1890, at the hour of 11 o'clock, A. M.

Not transferable.

CHARLES YUND,

Sheriff Albany County.

George Black on the scaffold; and the invitation to the execution.

American Heritage Center University of Wyoming

Black retired at 12:50 a.m. and spent a restless night. He arose at 6:00 a.m. when he was awakened by the changing of the guard. Father Hugh Cummiskey arrived next and was with Black a good part of the morning, and Benjamin Black and their three sisters joined them for a while. Deputy Sheriff Alex McKay visited and pleaded with Black, for the sake of his soul, to tell the truth, but the condemned man continued to insist that he was innocent. The prisoner had his breakfast at 9:30 a.m. and this seemed to brace him for the ordeal. He dressed in a new black suit and kept his derby hat at hand. Special deputies were then admitted in small groups, and Black's last visitors, three women, came and went.

The scaffold had been erected within a twenty-by-twenty foot shed at the rear of the jail. At 11:00 a.m. Father Cummiskey started from the cell with the prisoner, a metal cross firmly gripped in Black's right hand, and Sheriff Yund following closely behind. The distance to the trap was only one hundred feet. The procession ascended but stopped a few feet from the trapdoor, where the priest offered a prayer, shook hands with Black, presented a cross for him to kiss, and then quickly retired. Fifty people watched as Black stepped onto the trapdoor, unassisted, and then Deputy McKay pinioned his arms and legs with straps. The sheriff placed, cinched, and adjusted the noose. He asked the prisoner if he had anything to say to the witnesses, but Black declined except to say, "I am not the one who did it." Sheriff Yund pulled the black cap from his pocket and placed it over the prisoner's head at 11:12 a.m. and in the next moment turned toward the release, gave the twine a firm tug, and the trap fell. The body dropped 8 feet, breaking the prisoner's neck.

Dr. T. Getty Ricketts of Carbon and Drs. J. H. Finfrock and Henry L. Stevens of Laramie stood on chairs; one monitoring the heartbeat while the other two each held a wrist and counted the pulse of the hanging figure. The condemned man's pulse ceased at six minutes, and life was pronounced extinct. Black's body was cut down at 11:39 a.m., twenty-seven minutes after he fell. Black's remains were placed in a cheap coffin provided by the county and slid into a one-horse hearse. He was buried in potter's field at county expense that afternoon.

Black had tried for months to murder Robert Burnett, or drive him off his land, and he finally succeeded in committing one of the most cold-blooded murders in Wyoming history. He coveted another man's land and was willing to do anything to get it.

The Johnson County War

The so-called Johnson County War has often included the lynching of Jim Averell and Ella Watson as the first skirmish, but that incident occurred in Carbon County. The next murderous action taken by the Wyoming Stock Growers Association (WSGA), also mistakenly included in that war, was the lynching of Tom Waggoner on or about June 4, 1891, but that murder took place in Weston County. The real Johnson County War, where more than seventy men were marked for death, only took two lives—those of Nate Champion and Nick Ray.

Nate Champion was alleged to be a cattle rustler and a marked target of the WSGA. His first run-in with the powerful WSGA was on November 1, 1891. A shoot-out between the two factions resulted in some injuries, but Champion escaped unscathed. This attack caused Champion to search for a safer place to live and, with Nick Ray, he leased the abandoned K-C Ranch in Johnson County.

Nathan D. "Nate" Champion was born near Round Rock, Texas, on September 29, 1857. As a young man he worked for several cattle ranchers and eventually, in about 1881, went north with a herd into Wyoming. He saw the potential of the region and decided to settle in Johnson County, taking jobs with several ranchers.

After the terrible blizzard of January 1887 decimated the herds, some cattle barons went broke and many cowboys were out of work. They survived by finding an abandoned place to call home, living off the land, and butchering a few stray cattle they jokingly called "slow elk" or "range elk." As the herds and the cattle barons began to recover over the next few years, cowboys like Champion staked out small pieces of land and began building their own small herds from the maverick cattle running loose on the open range. This resulted in the passage of the

Frank Canton was one of the leaders of the Johnson County invasion.
Wyoming State Archives Department of State Parks and Cultural Resources

Maverick Law in 1890, which stated that all unbranded cattle on the open range belonged to members of the WSGA.

By 1891 Champion had built a herd of several hundred head of mavericks. This herd of cattle, which the remaining cattle barons believed belonged to them, put him at odds with the WSGA and brought an informal charge of rustling in accordance with the Maverick Law. Champion's friend, Nick Ray, came to Wyoming with a herd of forty thousand cattle and settled in Johnson County. Like Champion, Ray was a cattle rustler in the eyes of the WSGA.

The cattle barons were determined to drive the homesteaders and rustlers off Johnson County's open range. They devised a plan to assemble an army, invade the county, and dispose of more than seventy men. They raised a fighting fund of one hundred thousand dollars and compiled a list of names that included both Champion and Ray. They gave the list to Frank Canton who, with ex-Army Officer Frank Wolcott and Tom Smith, rode to Texas to hire gunmen. They offered the hired guns five dollars per day plus expenses and a fifty bonus for each kill. A force of twenty-six men was hired.

The gunman arrived in Cheyenne on the morning of April 5 aboard a chartered Union Pacific train. At Cheyenne the force was joined by men hired from the northern part of the state and also a physician and two newspaper reporters, bringing the force to more than fifty men.

At 6:00 p.m. the small army took the train to Casper. Their first designated destination on their invasion was Buffalo, the county seat of Johnson County. Buffalo was the stronghold of the small ranchers while Sheridan had become the county's center for the cattle barons. At Buffalo, Sheriff "Red" Angus was in charge and he and his deputies, along with another thirty men of Buffalo, were on the list in Canton's pocket. The plan was that, following the killing of the authorities in Buffalo, the WSGA would set up a puppet government to do their bidding. However, during the 100-mile trip northward, Wolcott and Canton learned that Nate Champion and Nick Ray were living at the old K-C

Ranch. It was decided, probably with strong encouragement by Canton, to detour and kill these two men first.

On the evening of April 8, two trappers, Ben Jones and Bill Walker, visited Champion and Ray. The four men spent the evening talking, drinking, and singing along with Walker's fiddle. In the morning Jones went out to fetch a pail of water, but he was taken prisoner by Wolcott's men, who had completely surrounded the cabin. They dragged Jones some distance from the cabin and, upon seeing that his name was not on the list, bound him and held him prisoner. In thirty minutes Walker went out to see what had detained Jones, and he too was taken prisoner. In a short while Ray stepped out of the cabin and was immediately shot down in a hail of gunfire. Champion came out firing two pistols, but the

The army that invaded Johnson County to murder the men falsely accused of rustling by the Wyoming Stock Grower's Association.

Wyoming State Archives Department of State Parks and Cultural Resources

heavy gunfire drove him back into the cabin. He came out again firing his guns but this time dragged Ray into the cabin. Ray bled to death at about 9:00 a.m. Champion kept up the fight all day, though he was wounded. During the battle he managed to write a detailed journal of the events of the day.

At 3:00 p.m. Jack Flagg, a friend of Champion and another name on WSGA's list, drove his wagon near the cabin. When fifty guns were turned on him, he fled, leaving the wagon behind. Flagg went to Buffalo and sounded the alarm, which prompted Sheriff Angus to gather a posse of over two hundred men to ride to the K-C Ranch, rescue Champion and Ray, and capture or kill the invaders.

Meanwhile, the attacking army took Flagg's wagon, piled it with brush and dry wood, lit it afire, and pushed it against the cabin. The fire soon engulfed the building and drove Champion out, still firing two revolvers at his attackers. He was caught in crossfire and gunned down, and after he fell the men still fired into his body to be sure he could never rise again. In all there were twenty-eight bullet wounds in Champion's body. Canton then pinned a note to Champion's shirt that read: cattle thieves, beware!

The WSGA army caught wind of Angus's posse, so they quickly fled to the deserted T. A. Ranch. There they prepared a defense.

When the posse reached the K-C Ranch, they found Champion's body riddled with bullets and Ray's body in the ashes of the cabin burned beyond recognition. The remains were collected and sent to Buffalo. The posse continued in pursuit of the WSGA army, and by the time Angus's posse reached the T. A. Ranch it had grown to over three hundred men.

The posse completely surrounded the main ranch building, where the invading army had quartered behind a log breastwork. Angus's men dug rifle pits and assembled other cover so that there was no chance for any of the invaders to escape. The original exchanges of gunfire slowly died out as neither force could move on the other from their safe positions.

On April 13, after the standoff had lasted three days, and just as the posse was about to unleash a mobile bomb to blow the invaders from the ranch house, three troops from the Sixth Cavalry at Fort McKinney arrived. Sheriff Angus requested that the invaders be put in his custody, but Colonel J. J. Van Horn refused to be a party to fifty hangings and escorted his prisoners to Cheyenne.

The cattle barons were in control in the Magic City of the Plains, so no one was ever charged with the murders of Champion or Ray. Nathan D. Champion and Nick Ray were buried in the Willow Grove Cemetery in Buffalo, Wyoming.

Once again the Wyoming Stock Growers Association had sent their agents to do their dastardly work. The WSGA "army" was returned to Cheyenne under escort of the Cavalry, where the WSGA controlled the government and the press. No charges were brought against anyone for the invasion or the two murders. The WSGA abandoned its plan to invade Johnson County, though the conflict with the small ranchers and homesteaders continued. Sheriff Angus disbanded his posse and returned to Buffalo, where he remained on constant alert. The WSGA remained in control for years, later going to war with the sheepherders and authorizing murders. The WSGA still exists today as a formidable political force in Wyoming.

Butch Cassidy and the Sundance Kid
Those Elusive "Wild Bunch" Boys

Robert Leroy Parker, best known as Butch Cassidy during the heyday of his criminal career, is among the half-dozen most elusive outlaws of the Old West—even in death. His only capture and imprisonment was in 1894 for a crime that he probably didn't commit, but by then Cassidy was already a confirmed desperado.

His first reported death occurred about May 14, 1898, near Price, Utah. On July 24, 1898, the *Salt Lake Tribune* reported: "The supply of Butch Cassidays [*sic*] seems inexhaustible. You will find him in every county of the state . . . several of him have been killed . . ." By 1903 Cassidy had been killed more than a dozen times. According to the *Vernal Times*, "He must have more lives than a whole family of cats." Cassidy continued to die over and over on three continents during the next forty-five years.

The most likely spot for the demise of Butch Cassidy, and his side-kick the "Sundance Kid," was in San Vicente, Bolivia, in 1908, though the date varies and is often reported as 1909 or 1911. Their death scene in San Vicente was made popular by the blockbuster movie titled with their aliases. Cassidy also died at least seven times in Argentina between 1904 and 1935, twice in Honduras, once each in Ecuador and Uruguay, and several times in Venezuela during the early 1900s. He only died twice in Europe, once of old age in Ireland and once murdered in Paris, France, about 1906.

In the United States there were many reports of Cassidy's death as well. Those reports include: eight deaths in various Nevada towns; six deaths in Utah; several deaths in Washington State, Oregon, and

Key members of the Wild Bunch included: [front row L to R] Harry Longabaugh (Sundance Kid), Ben Kilpatrick, George Leroy Parker (Butch Cassidy); [back row L to R] Will Carver, Harvey Logan. *Denver Public Library, Western History Collection, Noah Rose/Z-49*

California; a death in Wyoming and one in Colorado after the turn of the twentieth century; and in the east one death in New York City and one somewhere in Georgia.

Harry A. "Sundance Kid" Longabaugh "died" only a few times in the United States, but he outlived his partner in crime. His death, after expiring with Cassidy all over South America, was reported first in Fort Worth, Texas, in 1954. Then he was reported dead in a Utah prison in 1955, in Oregon in 1956, in Montana in 1957, and finally in Wyoming in 1967.

The deaths of popular outlaws are often disputed, even when there is indisputable evidence, so it is no surprise that the reported deaths of

The Hole-in-the-Wall hideout was never breached by Wyoming lawmen.
Wyoming State Archives Department of State Parks and Cultural Resources

Butch Cassidy and the Sundance Kid are controversial and numerous. However, the lives and criminal careers of most of Wyoming's "Wild Bunch" outlaws have been well documented, making Cassidy and Sundance the notable exceptions to the rule.

The Wild Bunch was aptly named. They were certainly wild by any standard, and they were also more of an assorted "bunch" than a "gang." The Wild Bunch was a coalition of individual desperadoes and small gangs that hid out at the Hole-In-the-Wall, which was located in a desolate part of Johnson County, Wyoming, where a wall of parallel hills ran for fifty miles. There was a gap, or "hole," on the east, which could be defended by a few men. No hideout would be safe without a "back door," and to the west of the Hole-in-the-Wall there were numerous trails out of the area providing the men an avenue for escape.

On any illegal outing the participants could include a number of different men from the Wild Bunch, and this may have been intentional as

81

lawmen often had to guess which members of the bunch had participated in a particular crime. At times there were one hundred to one hundred and fifty wanted men hiding at Hole-in-the-Wall, and any of them could be recruited for a particular job. Those "jobs" took them to various parts of the southwest, including Colorado, Montana, Arizona, and Nevada, where the Wild Bunch engaged in rustling horses and cattle, robbing banks, and holding up stagecoaches and trains.

Robert Leroy Parker, one of the most famous gang members, was born in Beaver, Utah, in 1866. He was still quite young when he left home after a minor skirmish with the law, more of a misunderstanding than a crime. He soon met Mike Cassidy, whose last name he would later adopt as his alias, and the two engaged in cattle rustling. In 1884 altered brands were discovered and the cattle were traced back to Parker. He fled and, to ensure that his family would not be shamed by his criminal activities, it was then he adopted the alias Butch Cassidy and went to Telluride, Colorado. He tried to follow the honest path of a teamster, but he was too restless to settle down. After a few months in Colorado, he moved on to Wyoming.

Cassidy befriended others interested in making quick, easy money, and in 1889 he and a small party rode to Telluride and robbed the San Miguel Bank. Cassidy laid low for several years after the Colorado bank robbery, but in 1894 he was arrested for stealing horses. He was tried, convicted, and sentenced to a two-year term at the prison near Laramie. Prison hardened Cassidy and there he became convinced that he needed to form a gang. After his release on January 19, 1896, he met Harry Longabaugh and, seeing no reason for delay, formed the "Wild Bunch." They robbed a bank in Utah and then in August robbed another bank in Montpelier, Idaho.

After the Idaho robbery, Sundance and Cassidy parted ways for awhile. During that time Sundance was involved in a number of train robberies. When Sundance and Cassidy reunited at the Hole-in-the-Wall in late 1898, Sundance shared his train robbery experiences with Cassidy. The men immediately began to plan an assault on a train.

Cassidy recruited a dozen men into a gang that came to be called the "Train Robber's Syndicate," virtually a gang within a gang. Their first train-robbing excursion was thwarted by an undercover lawman. Cassidy would next plan to rob a train at Wilcox, Wyoming.

Cassidy, in planning the Wilcox train robbery, knew that posses would be on their trail quickly, so he developed a system of horse relays so that his men would always have fresh horses for their getaway. For days before a robbery, Cassidy would scout the region for good horse-flesh, building a string that was bred for endurance and very fast over short distances. He would place the horses at the place of the robbery and along the escape route. When in place, Cassidy would see to it that all the horses were pampered for days before the robbery took place.

At 2:00 a.m. on June 2, 1899, two men waving lanterns on the tracks motioned the Union Pacific train No. 1 to stop at milepost 609, one mile west of Wilcox, Wyoming. There was a small wooden bridge up ahead and engineer W. R. Jones thought it might have washed out. An engineer could not jeopardize his train by ignoring an emergency signal, so Jones brought his train to a halt.

Two men, masked and armed, boarded the engine. Next they gained entrance to the express car and safe. The contents were quickly removed and the robbers disappeared into the darkness. Later their trail revealed that they had horses tied a short distance away and rode north toward Casper. The trainmen could not identify any of the robbers, but deduced that Cassidy, Harvey "Kid Curry" Logan, and "Flat Nose" George Curry were involved along with other members of the Wild Bunch. It was supposed that the men got very little, as there was not much in the safe. Rewards of three thousand dollars per man ensured that there would be many large posses in the field, and it was estimated that nearly four hundred men participated in the pursuit at different times and places. However, the robbers were never captured for the robbery.

As anticipated by Cassidy, posses took to the field in great strength and with all due speed. The day following the robbery a Union Pacific special train arrived at Casper with Converse County's Sheriff Josiah Hazen, fresh horses, and men. A local rancher, Al Hudspeth, reported that three fugitives were camped at Casper Creek 6 miles northwest of town and they had run him off at gunpoint when he stopped to visit. When he described the men, the lawmen knew they were Harvey Logan, "Flat Nose" George Curry, and Elza Lay. Inquiries were made and it was determined that the three men had stopped in Casper to buy supplies. Hazen called for reinforcements, and a posse of twenty men set out to capture the three train robbers.

The posse took the field Monday and from Casper Creek followed the trail to within 5 miles of the horse ranch at Salt Creek. They had proceeded only a few hundred yards past that point when Curry shot and killed posse man Tom McDonald. Oscar Heistant, Sheriff of Natrona County, had his horse shot from under him by one of the robbers during a withering fusillade, so Heistant was sent afoot to the nearest ranch with orders to bring back more men.

The three fugitives and the reinforced posse continued a running gun battle throughout the day, but the fugitives managed to escape. On Tuesday, Sheriff Hazen and Dr. J. F. Leeper came to a draw and dismounted to look for a trail. Just as Hazen called to Leeper that he had found the tracks, Harvey Logan stood up from his hiding place behind a boulder, took careful aim, and shot the sheriff in the stomach. The three fugitives kept up the fire for a short time, but when the rest of the posse came up they mounted and fled again. Hazen was taken back to Casper and then by special train to Douglas, where he died at 5:00 a.m. on Tuesday.

The killing of Hazen outraged Wyoming's citizens, and a hundred trackers were dispatched to look for a trail. The U.S. marshal organized a posse of fifteen handpicked deputies, and bloodhounds were put on the scent. The governor mobilized the state militia, and more than a hundred men volunteered for posse service. Even with all this effort and large rewards, the three train robbers managed to elude capture and escaped the region.

The Wild Bunch took fourteen months off before returning to Wyoming, waiting for interest in the huge rewards to wane. Finally on August 29, 1900, they were ready to rob another train. One of the robbers slipped aboard the blind baggage of Union Pacific's train No. 3 as it pulled out of Tipton, Wyoming, located midway between Rawlins and Rock Springs in Sweetwater County. The robber climbed over the tender and took the engineer and fireman hostage at gunpoint. When the train was two and a half miles west of Tipton, he ordered the train to stop, and three other robbers appeared from the shadows. They began shooting their pistols along the sides of the passenger cars to prevent any interference and, when they felt secure, they went to the express car and forced their way in by threatening to dynamite the car. E. C. Woodcock, the same messenger they had robbed at Wilcox, opened the door and gave no resistance.

The Wild Bunch used too much explosive and destroyed the baggage car, the safe, and the contents in the Wilcox Station train robbery. *Union Pacific Museum*

As soon as they were inside, they placed a large charge of Kepauno Chemical Company's Giant Powder on the through safe and blew it apart, along with most of the express car. The amount taken was later disputed. The Pacific Express Company reported a loss of $50.40, but Woodcock said he carried $55,000, and Cassidy later said they had taken $45,000. There was $3,000 worth of damage done to the express car.

On the run, the gang buried the treasure, believing for some reason that it could be traced to them. Then the group rode to Huntington, Nevada. The railroad and the express company offered a reward of $1,000 for each man for a total of $8,000, but the robbers again eluded lawmen.

The Tipton robbery convinced the railroad that they needed to do something to stop the robberies of their trains in Wyoming. Recognizing the efficient getaway method that Cassidy developed using relays of fresh horses, the railroad started dispatching special horse car trains to the scene as soon as a robbery was reported. One month after robbing the train near Tipton, the men who had fled into Nevada robbed the bank at Winnemucca. Then, once again, the Bunch laid low until interest cooled. In late June 1901 three men including Cassidy, Logan, Ben Kilpatrick, and Laura Bullion went to Wagner, Montana, to rob a train. Wagner and the Great Northern Railroad had been chosen because the Union Pacific was then using those special horse cars and posses for speedy pursuits in Wyoming.

This was to be Cassidy's final robbery in North America, and he planned to flee to South America with a big haul. There he planned to rendezvous with Sundance, who was already aboard a ship bound for Argentina in the company of Etta Place. They recruited O. C. "Deaf Charley" Hanks, a Montana train robber, and on July 3, 1901, Kilpatrick boarded as a passenger in Malta while Logan slipped onto the blind baggage. When the train neared Exeter Switch, 3 miles east of Wagner, Logan climbed over the tender and captured engineer Tom Jones and his fireman at gunpoint. The other two robbers were waiting on the tracks and waved a flag to signal the place to stop the train. The two out-side men fired their pistols along the sides of the cars to keep the pas-sengers from interfering, but several shots were too close and ricocheted into the cars causing several minor wounds.

The robbers broke into the express car and blew open the safe, which contained $40,000 in bank notes sent to the Montana National Bank in Helena. The plunder was loaded onto horses, and the four rob-bers rode south across the Milk River and turned east. After four days following their trail, lawmen said they believed that the fugitives were better mounted than any of the posses and were probably somewhere between the Missouri River and the Hole-in-the-Wall. The Great Northern Express Company offered a five thousand dollar reward for their arrest and $500 for each conviction. The company circulated descriptions, and all but Cassidy were captured, convicted, and sen-tenced to prison terms.

As planned, Cassidy booked passage to South America and joined Sundance. There he tried to live an honest life as a rancher. It was gen-erally believed that he later returned to a life of crime, which led to his death in that San Vicente cantina, or perhaps he returned to the United States or Europe under an alias and lived out his life in relative obscu-rity—"dying a thousand deaths" here and there.

Of all the outlaws in Wyoming's rich criminal history, Butch Cassidy and the Sundance Kid are its best-known habitual criminals—outlaws in every respect. They were wild, but also careful planners, and commit-ted more than a dozen successful robberies of banks and trains after they graduated from petty thievery and rustling. Cassidy had been arrested a half-dozen times during his early career but was only con-victed twice before maturing into an armed robber. Sundance was con-victed only once, surprisingly spending his time in a local jail for a serious offense. Where and when these elusive outlaws died will proba-bly never be determined but, even if the law never expiated their crimes, time eventually overtakes everyone.

John "Badeye" Santamarazzo
The Weston County Poisoner

In the 1814 book *Traité de Toxicologie*, Mathew J. B. Orfila wrote:

> Revolted by the odious crime of homicide, the chemist's aim is to perfect the means of establishing proof so that the heinous crime (of poisoning) will be brought to light and proved to the magistrate, who must punish the criminal.

In the Old West, deadly weapons of all types were readily available to anyone who wanted them. The most common weapons included rifles, shotguns, pistols, axes, and knives. Other dangerous weapons were available based upon a man's occupation, and miners had access to picks, shovels, sledges, and all sorts of tools and materials that could be used to kill another person. Therefore, with all of these readily available weapons, it was surprising when a man resorted to poison as a means to bring about another man's death.

Nonetheless, this seemed to occur about once every ten years between 1887 and 1906. In 1887 Frederick Hopt from Utah asked a druggist to supply him with strychnine "to kill the rats which are eating my grain at camp." The druggist refused to supply him with the poison, and so Hopt returned to camp and bludgeoned John F. Turner to death. Twenty years later in Montana, Miles Fuller put strychnine in Henry Callahan's sugar bowl in the hope that he would eat the poison and die, leaving his land vacant for Fuller to occupy. Callahan must have noticed the tampering and did not eat the poison. In his defense, Fuller would

John Santamarazzo used poison to try to murder his enemy.
Wyoming State Archives Department of State Parks and Cultural Resources

later claim, "I know too much about poison for that purpose and recommend arsenic." In another incident John Santamarazzo tried to use strychnine to kill a man with whom he had a dispute. Like the others, he too failed to kill his victim with poison.

John Santamarazzo was born in Italy in 1843. He came to America as a youth and traveled west, settling in Wyoming by the mid-1890s. He had been a miner all his life and found work in the coalmines of Weston County in northeast Wyoming. In August 1895 he was fifty-three years old. He was "married but without children" and described as "poorly educated, about five feet eight inches tall and weighing one hundred and sixty pounds, with long black hair and black eyes, 'white' but with a very dark complexion," according to Elnora L. Frye's work on the prisoners at Wyoming's Territorial Prison.

Santamarazzo's appearance was rugged, and he looked like a true outlaw. He had been injured in a mine explosion during his earlier mining days and it had left him with powder burn discoloration on the left side of his face and ear. His left eyelid drooped over a blind eye, earning him the sobriquet "Badeye." He had led a somewhat violent life as evidenced by a cut scar in the middle of his forehead, another on his left arm, another large cut on his "short ribs," and an "ax mark" on his left arm.

In April 1895, Santamarazzo was working for the Cambria Mine. There he met Mike Dancy (sometimes spelled Dacy, Dacey, and Darcy), who was a teamster at the mine. Dancy and Santamarazzo had a heated argument on August 13, but it failed to escalate to violence; still, the ill-tempered and vindictive Italian swore he would kill Dancy.

The following afternoon Dancy took his dinner break with Santamarazzo, Theodore Shaw, Freeman Fossler, Charles Isem, and Henry Sulzner. He opened his meal bucket and took a large bite of bread, and then remarked to his companions that it had a "strong bitter taste to the first mouthful." Immediately, Dancy's neck began to stiffen in an awkward position. Before he could speak another word, he collapsed and was immediately overcome by violent spasms. His body jack-knifed back and forth, and he groaned in agony. The slightest noise or vibration on the floor aggravated the symptoms and caused the convulsions to become even more severe.

Once summoned, Dr. George Garrison Verbryck rushed Dancy to the nearby hospital for treatment. Dancy's dinner bucket was also collected and turned over to the doctor, because there appeared to be foul play. Upon examination Verbryck found a colorless, crystalline powder sprinkled throughout the food. The doctor identified the substance as strychnine and determined there was enough of the poison present to kill a hundred men.

Fortunately for Dancy, the bitter taste had caused him to pause in eating his meal and have a conversation with his fellow workers. This had prevented him from ingesting a fatal dose. The doctor managed to pump his stomach and administer activated charcoal, which soon revived the patient. Still, it took a short while before the victim could talk. When he was able to speak, he stated that he did not know who could have tried to kill him. He knew of no enemy who would want to take his life, "unless it was that Italian who I argued with yesterday. He said he would kill me."

Sulzner, who was at the meal table that day, would later testify that he observed Santamarazzo "when Dancy first took ill and saw actions and expressions of the Itallion [sic]…and believed M. Dancy received poison at the hands of Santamarazzo." Others said they had seen Santamarazzo lurking around the meal buckets earlier in the day.

On the afternoon of August 14, 1895, Weston County Sheriff John Owens filed a criminal complaint before Justice of the Peace P. J. Welsh. The complaint charged that "J. Santamarazzo…[tried] to take the life of Mike Daucey [sic] by distributing poison in his lunch and victuals with the intention of poisoning the same." Dancy also filed a criminal complaint charging that Santamarazzo "…did willfully, maliciously and unlawfully administer poison with the intent to kill the said

Mike Dancy." The judge issued a warrant based upon the complaints and, upon receiving it, the sheriff immediately served it on the suspected poisoner, arresting him and lodging him in the Weston County Jail in Newcastle.

On April 4, 1896, Sheriff Owens took Santamarazzo from jail to the court, where counsel was appointed. Since the defendant could not adequately speak or understand the English language, the court provided an interpreter. On April 20, 1896, Wyoming's Fourth Judicial District Court convened and heard the testimony of several witnesses, including the four men that were present and Dr. Verbryck.

Theodore Shaw testified, "I was present and witnessed the condition of M. Dacey [*sic*] and saw that he had spasms and that I examined the dinner pail and contents and could see something resembling strychnine in the bread, and Dr. Verbryck made an examination of the food and found strychnine freely distributed in the food"; Freeman Fossler testified next and stated that Dancy "had spasms resembling that of a man having taken poison" and said he believed it was "administered by the hands of the accused prisoner." Charles Isem swore that "I was present…and saw the condition and action of M. Dancy after he had eaten his dinner and saw the food containing strychnine." Lastly, Henry Sulzner testified to the same and to the guilty appearance of Santamarazzo's countenance and demeanor. The doctor testified to the type of poison, its presence in the food, the symptoms of Dancy, and the treatment for strychnine poisoning that had been successful in reviving the victim.

An indictment charged the defendant with two counts. The first stating that: "Santamarazzo…unlawfully, willfully, maliciously and feloniously…administered poison—to wit: strychnine—to one Mike Dacy [*sic*], with intent to kill him…death not ensuing there from, contrary to the form upon the Statute in such case made and provided, and against the peace and dignity of the State of Wyoming." The indictment's second count read, "…and the said L. T. Griggs, County and prosecuting attorney…informs the Court and gives the Court to understand, that the same (Santamarazzo) did unlawfully, willfully, maliciously, feloniously… mingle poison—to wit: strychnine—with food of one Mike Dacy [*sic*], with intent to kill him…death not ensuing there from."

Santamarazzo was arraigned and a jury was quickly empanelled. The same counsel that had represented him at the arraignment was appointed to represent him at trial. The case began before noon on the April 19, and the presentation of evidence occupied the remainder of that day and the next. The case went to the jury shortly before 9:00 p.m. The jury could not arrive at a verdict and remained in the jury room overnight, but in the morning the foreman told the judge that they were hopelessly deadlocked—eight for conviction and four for acquittal. The jury was dismissed and a second jury empanelled.

Santamarazzo was then arraigned on a charge of "the crime of attempt to kill with poison," which was a slight change in the wording from the first trial. The testimony was again taken on April 21, and the case went to the jury late on the second day, but again this jury could not arrive at a swift verdict and spent the night in the jury room. Deliberations continued throughout the following day. At 4:00 p.m. John P. Ost, jury foreman, announced, "We the jury…do find the defendant…guilty as charged in the Information." The prisoner was then remanded to the county sheriff to be held in the jail until sentence was passed.

Within a few days, on April 28, 1896, the prisoner was brought into court again. The former coalminer was sentenced to serve nine years in the penitentiary near Laramie. On May 5, 1896, the prisoner was delivered from the Newcastle jail to the prison by Weston County's Sheriff John Owens. He was registered in the Bertillon Book as convict #258.

Santamarazzo was at the Laramie prison, known as the Territorial Prison, when the new state prison, called the Frontier Prison, was opened in Rawlins. He was in the fourth group of convicts transferred there on December 21, 1901. On June 23, 1904, by reason of "expiration of sentence," authorities released Santamarazzo on his earliest release date, having awarded him 460 days of good time credit as required under the Goodwin Act. His release date would have been April 27, 1905, without the credit for good time.

Good police work and the willingness of witnesses to testify led to the arrest, trial, and conviction of John Santamarazzo before he could commit another crime. His disdain for the life of another man suggests that if he had succeeded in killing Mike Dancy, he would not have hesitated to commit another crime. He may have again chosen the diabolical and unique method of poisoning.

Charles F. Woodard
The Murderer of Sheriff Ricker

In December 1901 property was stolen from Charles Francis Woodard's neighbor in Garfield Park, seventy-five miles west of Casper. The neighbor had reason to suspect Woodard, a man of dubious character, so in late December the neighbor filed a complaint. Charles and his brother Clarence were arrested for the theft and taken to Casper. Clarence had been arrested in 1896 for stealing a horse and spent two-and-a-half years in prison for the offense, but Charles was thought to be the worst of the brothers and involved in all manner of shady dealings, though never convicted of any particular crime.

On the night of December 31, Charles Woodard, anticipating a conviction for the crime of burglary or grand theft and a hefty prison sentence, obtained a six-inch-long hacksaw blade. With some difficulty, he managed to saw his way out of jail as well as that of his brother Clarence and prisoners Thomas Jeff Franklin and James Westfall. After gaining their freedom the men secured horses and headed for the Woodard ranch at Garfield Peak.

Clarence Woodard and Franklin took one trail while Charles Woodard and Westfall took another. Clarence and Franklin were quickly captured. Clarence was convicted of burglary on January 25, 1902, and sentenced to serve three years in prison. Franklin was convicted of aiding in the escape and, on February 13, 1902, was sentenced to serve a three-year prison term.

Meanwhile, the other two escapees were still on the run. On their way to the ranch, the two were separated and Westfall arrived at the ranch a day ahead of Charles. The morning following the jailbreak, a

Charles F. Woodard escalated a simple theft case to first-degree murder.

Frances Seely Webb Collection

posse left Casper and (comprising Sheriff W. C. "Charlie" Ricker of Natrona County and two deputies) arrived at the Woodard ranch early on the evening of January 2, 1902, and found James Westfall awaiting the arrival of Charles. They arrested the fugitive and took over the house to wait for Charles.

Woodard arrived that night and realized that the posse must be in the house with Westfall, laying in ambush for him. He went to the stable and found the posse's horses and Westfall's horse. Keeping the best horse for his getaway, Woodard drove off the others. He then returned to the barn and laid in wait for the officers to expose themselves.

Sheriff Ricker heard some noise, which aroused his suspicions, and decided to go to the barn alone and investigate, against the advice of his deputies. As he crossed the yard, he saw someone in the stable and called out, "Is that you Harry?" Perhaps he thought it was another posse member coming to their aid. Charles Woodard replied, "No, it isn't Harry," and fired a single shot causing a mortal wound.

The sheriff collapsed in the yard, unable to move. He lay quiet for some time and finally cried out that he was dying and begged for someone to come to his assistance. The deputies, who were still under cover inside the house, asked Woodard for permission to go to the sheriff, but the request was refused. One deputy remained in the ranch house to guard Westfall while the second deputy slipped out the back door, caught one of the horses that had been driven off by Woodard, and rode hard for Casper to get help.

Meanwhile, Woodard dragged the body of Sheriff Ricker into the barn and, finding life in him, took the officer's gun and beat him until life was extinct. He then robbed the dead sheriff of his watch and money. After killing the sheriff the murderer mounted his horse and fled north toward Montana, where he had friends he was certain would assist him.

A new posse was formed and started out after Charles Woodard, spending twenty-five days in pursuit. He was seen twice during that time, once being almost overtaken by Deputy Sheriff John Grieve, but

Sheriff Ricker was killed by Woodard, who tried to avoid being rearrested for a minor crime.

Eileen Hayes Skibo

in the running gun battle that followed, the deputy's horse was shot from under him, and Woodard fled.

Woodard went to the ranch of William Owens, thirteen miles from Billings, Montana. He identified himself as Bill Gad, and said he had some trouble in Wyoming. Owens allowed him to stay at his ranch—until he read in the newspaper the details of the murder. The description of the fugitive matched his guest, so he sent to Billings for handcuffs, which reached him on January 27.

At 1:00 p.m. that day Owens, a hired hand, and Woodard were all in the house. Suddenly, Woodard unbuckled and laid-off his two revolvers. Once the fugitive was unarmed, Owens and his hired hand tried to make the arrest, but a terrible fight ensued. The two men finally overpowered Woodard and cuffed him. He begged piteously for them to give him a running start so they could "shoot him down like a dog." He did not want to go back to jail. At that point he freely admitted to being Charles Woodard, the man wanted for the murder of Sheriff Ricker. Owens and others involved in the capture would later share in the one thousand dollar reward posted by Natrona County.

The authorities, fearing a lynching, asked the citizens of Casper for assurance that they would take no action against Woodard when he was returned. The citizens agreed, and Woodard was brought to Casper and lodged in jail.

On February 18, three weeks after his capture, Charles Woodard's trial for murder began before Judge Charles W. Bramel, a "no nonsense" judge. The trial lasted three days and was highlighted by Woodard's own testimony detailing how he killed the sheriff. In his testimony, he claimed it had been an accident. He stated that he saw someone approaching and so he pointed his gun at the person, at which point it had gone off unintentionally. He never explained who beat and robbed the wounded man.

At 11:00 p.m. on February 21, the jury, after an hour's deliberation and five ballots, returned a verdict of guilty of first-degree murder. On February 24 Judge Bramel pronounced Woodard's sentence:

Wretched and deluded man; in vain you have attempted to escape the consequences of your act; in vain you have ridden through the winter storms to elude the vigilance of your pursuers; in vain have you attempted to impress upon the hearts of twelve good and true men who sat upon your trial that you should have clemency.

One can almost see the hand of God in the weaving together of the remarkable chain of evidence that makes your escape from the punishment that awaits you impossible.

The sword of human justice trembles over you and is about to fall upon your guilty head. You are about to take your final leave of this world and enter upon the untried retribution of a never ending eternity. And I beg of you do not delude yourself with the vain hope of pardon or executive clemency which can never be realized. Your destiny for this world is fixed, and your fate inevitable.

Let me therefore entreat you, by every motive temporal and eternal, to reflect upon your present situation and the certain death that surely awaits you.

There is but one who can pardon your offenses: your creator. Let me therefore entreat you to fly to him for that mercy and that pardon which you must not expect from mortals.

When you have returned to the solitude of your prison, where you will be permitted to remain for a few short weeks let me entreat you by all that is still dear to you in time, by all that is dreadful in the retribution of eternity, that you seriously reflect upon your present situation and upon the conduct of your past life. Bring to your mind the horror of that dreadful night when the soul of the murdered sheriff was sent unprepared into the presence of his God, where you must shortly meet it as an accusing spirit against you.

Bring to your recollection the mortal struggles and dying groans of the man who had been kind to you and yours. Think of the situation of your wife, and your aged mother who nursed you in the lap of affection and watched over the tender years of your infancy. Then think of the widow and orphan children of the murdered sheriff, left alone as they are to battle the storm of life by your hand, and when by such reflections as these your heart shall have become softened, let me again entreat you, before your blood stained hands are raised in unavailing supplication before the judgment seat of Christ that you fly for mercy to the arms of the savior and endeavor to seize upon the salvation of the cross.

Listen now to the dreadful sentence of the law and then farewell, forever, until the court and you shall meet together in the land from whence no man returneth.

You, Charles Francis Woodard are to be taken from hence to the county jail of this county, and therein confined, under proper guard as provided by law, until the 28th day of March, 1902 at which time between the hours of 9 a.m. and 3 p.m. you are to be taken to an enclosure, especially prepared within the jail yard of said county, and that at said time and place you are to be hanged by your neck until you are dead.

And may that God whose laws you have broken and before whose tribunal you must then appear, have mercy on your soul.

Woodard's attorney, C. De Bennett, assured everyone that he was not going to file an appeal. However, as the time for the execution neared he went to Cheyenne, appeared at the state's supreme court, and tried to save the life of his client. He filed a petition of error and a motion for a stay of execution. On Tuesday, March 25, 1902, the supreme court granted a respite to Woodard to allow time to review the record of trial.

Concurrent to Woodard's case, two other murderers were awaiting execution. They too had lengthened their time in jail by various legal maneuvers and technicalities. Tom Horn was under the sentence of death in Cheyenne for the killing of Willie Nickell, a fourteen-year-old boy, and J. P. Walters was being held for the cold-blooded murder of a woman in Thermopolis. The people of Wyoming were frustrated by the law, and in Casper where outrage over the murder of their sheriff was still strong, the people were determined to see swift justice.

On Thursday afternoon a large number of men from the surrounding country, who were unaware of the respite, filed into Casper to witness Woodard's hanging. The talk of the town since Tuesday was the respite, and it was as much a surprise to these newcomers to town as it had been to the city's residents. The snow had been falling steadily, so the men gathered in the warmth of the saloons and hotels to discuss the matter.

It was fifteen minutes past midnight on the date set for Woodard's execution when the deputy sheriff at the jail was aroused by a hard knock on the door. He asked, "Who is there?" The reply was, "The Marshal with a prisoner." When the deputy opened the door the guns of twenty-eight masked men immediately covered him. He was searched, thrown to the floor, bound, and taken into his room, where a guard was posted.

The remainder of the men proceeded to Woodard's cell with the keys that they had found in the deputy's coat pocket. Deathwatch guard Samuel Erbin was on duty in the jail corridor. He was covered with guns through every opening and, as ordered, stepped back and lowered his head. The men entered and opened the door to Woodard's cell, and all had been done so quietly that they had to awaken him. Woodard, wearing only a shirt, asked to dress, but one of the lynchers said, "Never mind your clothes, you won't freeze to death."

By midnight there had appeared no organized effort to lynch Woodard, but still the persistent newsmen decided to go to the jail one last time before retiring. When they arrived they found masked men at the door to the jail. The newsmen were warned, "Hands up; depart; you have no business here, leave while you can." The newsmen identified themselves and were told, "Relate truthfully all that you see; but interfere and that act will be your last."

The mob took their prisoner out and escorted him to the enclosure inside which the gallows was built, where they knocked down the door. When the prisoner passed the newsmen, Woodard said, "Let them put this in the newspapers." The lynchers walked Woodard onto the scaffold, which had been erected for his execution later that day. When Woodard realized that the men meant to hang him he said, "Tell my little wife that my last words were for her. Tell her that, boys, won't you?"

The men were preparing the noose as Woodard directed them, "Make the noose a little longer, boys." He next begged to be allowed to pray, saying, "Boys, let me kneel and pray for you. I want to pray for all of you," but he was ignored. The loose end of the rope was thrown over the beam and when it was pulled taut Woodard cried out, showing fear for the first time. He said, "To my blessed little wife. Tell my dear little wife I love her dearly. Won't you tell her that, boys? I pray that you have the papers print a good article. I pray for myself. I pray for you and for Charles Ricker. I never had a grudge against him in God's world."

The release mechanism of the trapdoor puzzled the lynchers, and during the delay Woodard spoke again: "Good bye everybody, may the Lord have mercy on my soul. Boys, make it a little longer than that, just a little. Don't choke me boys. Let me tell you once more before I die that

I never shot Ricker purposely. Good bye. God have mercy on me and you, boys."

"Why did you kill him then?" one of the men asked, and the condemned man replied,

I never meant to kill him. Don't choke me boys. For God's sake, you're choking me, boys. Oh, God have mercy on me. God, have mercy on me and save me, and I pray for my blessed little wife. Don't choke me to death, boys. You are choking me. Please don't choke me. I didn't shoot Charlie Ricker on purpose. Lord have mercy on me and my dear little wife.

Several of the men, becoming frustrated by the trapdoor release and the constant whining, seized Woodard and threw him over the railing that surrounded the scaffold. The distance he fell was not adequate to break his neck. He was hanging there and rubbing against the side of the scaffold. The rope had not closed tightly on Woodard's throat, and he started convulsing. As he slowly strangled to death, he made terrible gasping sounds. Finally two men sprang forward and, taking the legs of the suspended man, pulled him down and away from the scaffold. With all of their weight they swung from Woodard's legs until life was extinct. One of the men announced, "The tax payers have had their say," as another man stepped forward and pinned a card on the dead man, which read:

Notice.
"Practice of law is a little slow,
so this is the road we have to go."
Murderers and thieves beware.
People's Verdict

As soon as the hanging was over, one of the members of the mob called out, "Scatter." Immediately, twenty-six men, and the two guarding the jail deputy, fled from the scene. At 1:40 a.m. the body was cut

The gallows on which Woodard was hanged. On the gallows L to R: Park C. Hayes, Sam W. Conwell, E. F. Seaver, unknown, Alfred J. Mokler, E. Tubbs (Sheriff), P. C. Nicolaysen. *Mokler Historical Collection Casper College Library*

down and taken to the town hall, where the rope was removed and cut into souvenirs. The sign was taken by one of the many spectators who had gathered after the hanging.

During the entire affair, Mrs. Woodard, who had arrived in Casper from Thermopolis the night before, was asleep in a nearby rooming house. She learned of her husband's death the next morning from the newspaper's special edition.

The coroner held an inquest the following morning, and the jury found that Woodard had died by hanging at the hands of persons unknown. At 2:00 p.m. on Saturday, March 29, the body of the murderer was interred in the cemetery at Casper. The widow paid for all expenses. Only twelve people were present at the graveside, all of them women who came for the sole purpose of comforting Mrs. Woodard.

Charles Woodard, like many an outlaw, began his career on the wrong side of the law with petty crimes. Once he was labeled a criminal, his offenses escalated until he committed a murder, in this case of a man elected and sworn to protect the public. A cop killer is was among the worst of the badmen in the Old West, and Woodard fit the bill exactly.

Tom Horn

The Cattle Detective

Tom Horn became one of Wyoming's most controversial outlaws. His status as a "cattle detective" appeared to many as a cover-up for his position as a paid assassin in the employ of the Wyoming Stock Grower's Association. As a serial killer, Horn had a unique calling card. He would place three rocks beneath the head of his victim, and this signature token made his murders easy to identify. Many wanted Horn dead, but many supported him as well. As a result, his murder conviction resulted in one of the most aggressive appeals processes known in the Old West.

Tom Horn was born into a large family in Franklin County, Missouri, in 1870. When he was a youngster, his father became a fugitive from the law for the crime of forgery. Tom left home and drifted to the southwest, making his living by driving bull teams into Texas and New Mexico. During his travels he earned a reputation as a "badman" when he killed a Mexican army officer over the affections of a girl. In New Mexico, Horn reportedly killed two sheepherders, but the law could never make the case so he was not arrested. While in New Mexico he joined the army as a scout and, in one instance, stood firm and fought off a gang of Mexicans and Indians single-handedly until his posse could rally to support him. As a scout he became close friends with Colonel W. F. "Buffalo Bill" Cody and General Nelson A. Miles.

Horn came to Wyoming Territory in 1894. He took a position as a cattle detective and rode the range intent on stopping cattle rustling. During that time, William Powell and William Lewis were murdered at their small ranches forty-five miles north of Cheyenne for being suspected of cattle rustling. Horn was a suspect in the murders, but a case against him was unsuccessful.

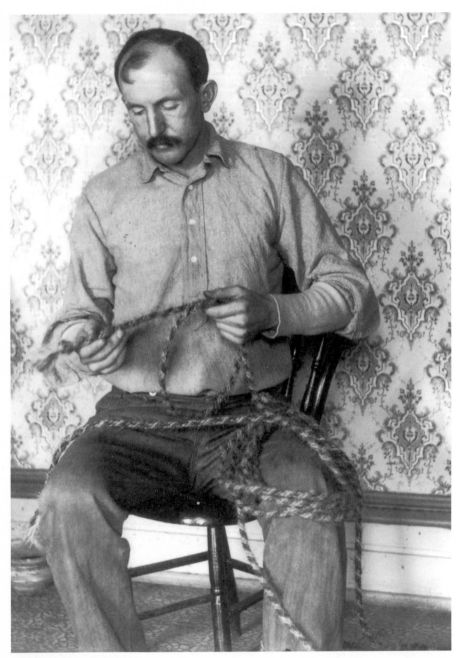

Tom Horn just before his execution.
Wyoming State Archives Department of State Parks and Cultural Resources

In 1898 Horn enlisted in the government's pack train service and went to Cuba during the Spanish-American War. He caught yellow fever soon after arriving there. When he returned to Wyoming Territory he showed the ravages of the disease, and it took him some months to regain his health.

On June 2, 1899, six robbers held up the Union Pacific train one mile west of Wilcox, Wyoming. Horn was well enough by then to take the trail in search of the large reward offered. After some time Horn returned to claim $4,000 of the reward for killing two of the robbers, whom he claimed to have buried where they had fallen. His story was suspicious, and so he led officers to the spot where he had buried the men and dug up the remains. The evidence showed that the two men he had killed were harmless prospectors whom he had shot from ambush without warning. He used to refer to that incident as his "funny mistake," but he was not arrested for the crime.

The next incident happened in 1900 when Matt Rash and Isham Dart, small ranchers in Brown's Hole County, Colorado, were assassinated within a short period of time of each other. Both of the men had been suspected of rustling. Horn was known to have been in the county when they were killed and had even eaten supper with Dart the night before his death. A posse went out to apprehend Horn. They didn't know what he looked like, and so Horn rode safely back into Wyoming unmolested. At Dixon, Wyoming, he stopped for a drink and became involved in a cutting affray with one of the posse members, who had also strayed into Wyoming. Horn received a severe cut on the back of his neck, which scarred noticeably.

In 1901 Horn was employed as a cattle detective for the Iron Mountain Ranch Company, which operated ranches at Bosler in Albany County and Iron Mountain in Laramie County. About this same time there was a feud between the Miller family and the Nickell family in the Iron Mountain district. The feud erupted when Kels P. Nickell brought sheep into cattle country. (Cattlemen believed that sheep ruined the grass and were determined to keep them off of "their" open range.)

At 7:00 a.m. on the morning of July 18, 1901, Willie Nickell, the fourteen-year-old son of Kels, was near the ranch wearing his father's coat and hat when he was shot in the back twice. He died instantly and, at first, the Millers were suspected. Three weeks later Kels Nickell was shot but managed to get into his house before being killed. He was taken into Cheyenne, treated, and he survived. He accused the Millers, Jim and Victor, of the shooting. However, Jim and his sixteen-year-old son proved an alibi and were released.

Horn had been seen in the vicinity a few days before Willie Nickell was murdered, but he could not be found after the killing. Horn finally turned up at the Bosler ranch and consented to testify at the inquest to establish his alibi. He gave a detailed account of his whereabouts at the time of the killing, and the coroner's jury again had to adjourn without a verdict.

In the meantime, U.S. Marshal Joe Lafors had been assigned to investigate the murder of Willie Nickell. He soon became convinced that Horn was responsible for Nickell's death, and devised a plan to get Horn to confess by relying on his love of liquor and reputation for boasting when drunk. In December 1901 Lafors had a friend write to Horn offering him a position in Montana that required him to go to Cheyenne and meet with Lafors to make the arrangements. Horn accepted and was soon on his way to Cheyenne, not knowing what lay ahead.

On January 12, 1902, Horn went to Lafors's office. He had been drinking heavily before he got there and Lafors further plied him with liquor. While Horn's inhibitions were low, the marshal got him to confess to the murder of the Nickell boy, and also got an admission to the killing of Powell and Lewis in 1894. In the next room Deputy Sheriff Les Snow and stenographer Charles Ohnhaus witnessed the confession, and Ohnhaus recorded the entire conversation. The following day Sheriff Ed J. Smalley and Undersheriff Richard A. Proctor arrested Horn.

Horn had his preliminary hearing in February and his trial was set for the May term of the district court, but his attorneys obtained a delay to the fall term. Horn's trial began on October 24, 1902, and after thirteen days of testimony the jury found him guilty of first-degree murder for the killing of Willie Nickel. A few days later Horn was sentenced to hang on January 9, 1903.

Then began one of the most aggressive appeals processes ever conducted in the history of the Old West. The execution was stayed as it took a year for the supreme court to consider the facts before affirming the lower court's decision. In October they rescheduled the execution of Horn for November 20, 1903. The fight for Horn's life next went to the governor, who was inundated with affidavits from both sides and with testimony of every sort. He even received a letter from a dying man saying he was guilty of the murder and would confess on his deathbed. On November 15 Governor Fenimore Chatterton refused to interfere.

There were many rumors that the jail would be attacked and Horn would be rescued, but the only incident that ever materialized was Horn's escape in August 1903. He was recaptured before he traveled two hundred yards. Although armed with a new automatic pistol, Horn had not learned how to release the safety and could not return fire. He was slightly wounded in the skirmish.

On Horn's last night he slept soundly and arose in excellent spirits. He asked for writing materials and spent the morning writing farewell letters, except for the few minutes he spent with his religious advisor Reverend G. C. Rafter and with his friend John C. Coble. He ate a hearty breakfast and enjoyed several cigars as he wiled away the last hours. He dressed in a red-striped shirt with low collar, a corduroy vest, black trousers, and gaiters.

At 9:00 a.m. the number of militiamen guarding the jail was greatly increased, and they formed a cordon around the building to keep back the growing crowd. Many spectators had taken up places in windows and on rooftops but they could see nothing of the scaffold. At 9:45 a.m.

a final test of the gallows was conducted and everything worked efficiently. The hearse from Gleason's Undertaking Parlor stood near the courthouse and attracted much attention from the crowd. At 10:55 a.m. the invited witnesses were admitted and they filed into the enclosure. Undersheriff Proctor walked to the gallows and arranged the straps and black cap on the railing, and then waited as the cell door was swung open.

Horn was brought out as far as the gangway and stopped. Then Charlie and Frankie Irwin sang a tune, which was a strange medley of railroad vernacular and sacred words, but it was inspiring. The two boys were summoned to the scaffold and they shook hands with Horn and told him to die game. When Charlie Irwin asked if he had confessed, Horn said, "No!"

When the singers left the platform, Proctor secured the straps about Horn's wrists and thighs as the condemned man joked with those in his procession. He was led onto the platform where he examined the trapdoor carefully and remarked, "I never saw one just like that before. I've seen several of them, but that is a new one." At 11:04 a.m. the noose was put over his head and he bent forward to help Proctor get it in place easily. His knees and ankles were then bound, and as the straps were cinched tight he was jerked a bit and said, "You're liable to tip me over here; somebody had better hold me. You fellows ought to have a handle on me so you could do this easier."

Reverend Rafter read a short passage from an Episcopal prayer book. As the reverend spoke Horn moved his head about as if the rope was uncomfortable, so Proctor stepped forward and lifted the heavy hangman's knot. While in that position Horn inspected the details of the knot. When the prayer finished at 11:06 a.m., Proctor lowered the knot and pulled the black cap over Horn's smiling face. The deputy asked, "Are you ready, Tom?" and he replied, "Yes!"

Sheriff Smalley and Joe Cahill lifted the condemned man onto the trapdoor. As he was being lifted he said, "Ain't gettin' nervous, are you?" and laughed through the cap. As soon as he was placed on the trap there

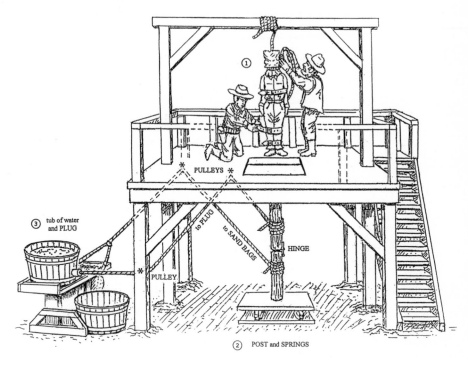

The "Julian" gallows on which Horn was hanged had a unique water-activated trigger system: 1) Horn, hooded and pinioned, lifted onto the trapdoor; 2) as post was depressed on eliptical springs, 3) it pulled plug from washtub; 4) when weight of water decreased, sandbags tipped lever and pulled post, releasing the trapdoor.
Eileen Hayes Skibo

was an audible "click" as his body weight activated a lever, which pulled a plug from a tub, filled with water, and it began to pour from the balance tank. When enough water had spilled out the counterweights fell, pulling the hinged post from beneath the trap.

Horn stood erect with his hands clenched tightly waiting for the trap to fall. It took thirty-five seconds before the post was pulled and the prisoner dropped through the trapdoor. Horn's neck was broken in the fall, but his heart continued to beat for sixteen minutes. He hung for another four minutes before being cut down and delivered to the man from Gleason's undertaking establishment. The next morning Horn's remains were shipped to Boulder, Colorado, in the custody of the deputy sheriff, for interment. The gallows was taken down the following day and stored in the courthouse barn in the event it would be needed again. It was later sent to the new prison at Rawlins when the responsibility for executions shifted from the county sheriff to the prison warden.

The facts suggest that Tom Horn was a serial killer for hire. He had killed many men for money, the deaths paid for by ranchers who were members of the Wyoming Stock Grower's Association. It is ironic that this cold-blooded killer would be arrested, tried, convicted, and hanged for a terrible crime—the murder of a young boy—for which he was most probably innocent.

But, Horn was an outlaw, a "cattle detective" who, for money, assassinated men marked by members of the WSGA. He did not seem to question whether his victims were actually rustlers or merely homesteaders who had taken up occupancy on prime rangeland. Horn took pride in his work by leaving a distinctive sign to boast that he was the killer. Finally, he was punished with an ignominious death for his reign of terror and his many assassinations.

Bibliography

General

Elman, Robert. *Badmen of the West*. Secaucus, NJ: Castle Books, 1974.

Gorzalka, Ann. *Wyoming's Territorial Sheriffs*. Glendo, WY: High Plains Press, 1998.

McLoughlin, Denis. *Wild and Woolly, an Encyclopedia of the Old West*. New York: Barnes & Noble, 1975.

Nash, Jay R. *Encyclopedia of Western Lawmen & Outlaws*. New York: Da Capo Press, 1994.

Thrapp, Dan L. *Encyclopedia of Frontier Biography*. University of Nebraska Press, 1988.

Urbanek, Mae. *Wyoming Place Names*. Missoula, MT: Mountain Press Publishing Co., 1988.

Wilson, R. Michael. *Crime & Punishment in Early Wyoming*. Unpublished manuscript, 2005.

————. *Murder & Execution in the Wild West*. Las Vegas: RaMA PRESS of Las Vegas, 2006.

Charles Martin and Charles Morgan: Hanged on the Tripod Gallows

Carroll, Murray L. "Judge Lynch Rides the Rails Bringing the Law to Laramie." *True West*, October 1995, p. 12.

Cheyenne (WY) Daily Leader: January 1, 1868; May 5, 1868; October 19–22, 1868.

Homsher, Lola M., ed. *South Pass, 1868: James Chisholm's Journal of the Wyoming Gold Rush.* Lincoln: University of Nebraska Press, 1960.

The Asa Moore Gang: Lynched by Vigilantes

Carroll, Murray L. "Judge Lynch Rides the Rails Bringing the Law to Laramie." *True West,* October 1995, p. 12.

Cheyenne (WY) Daily Leader: January 22, 1868; May 6, 1868; October 19–22, 1868.

Engebretson, Doug. *Empty Saddles, Forgotten Names: Outlaws of the Black Hills and Wyoming.* Aberdeen, SD: North Plains Press, 1984.

Gorzalka, Ann. *Wyoming's Territorial Sheriffs.* Glendo, WY: High Plains Press, 1998.

Attack of the Monitor

Brown, Mabel E. "Robbery at Canyon Springs." *Bits and Pieces,* May 1965, p. 2.

Cheyenne (WY) Daily Leader: September 25–26, 1878; September 28–29, 1878; October 1–6, 1878; October 10–11, 1878; October 17–18, 1878; October 25–26, 1878; November 5, 1878.

Engebretson, Doug. *Empty Saddles, Forgotten Names: Outlaws of the Black Hills and Wyoming.* Aberdeen, SD: North Plains Press, 1982.

McClintock, John S. *Pioneer Days in the Black Hills.* Norman: University of Oklahoma Press, 2000.

Randall, Arthur G. "Early Exploration of the Black Hills Area, Wyoming–South Dakota." *Wyoming Geological Association Guidebook,* p. 17.

Spring, Agnes W. *The Cheyenne and Black Hills Stage and Express Routes.* Lincoln: University of Nebraska Press, 1948.

"Big Nose" George Parrott and His Boys

Arlandson, Lee. "When 'Big Nose' George Parrott Was Hung." *Pioneer West,* June 1972, p. 40.

Breihan, Carl W. "Big Nose George Parrott." *Real West,* September 1968, p. 26.

Cheyenne (WY) Daily Leader: January 7, 1879; March 23, 1881.

Engebretson, Doug. *Empty Saddles, Forgotten Names: Outlaws of the Black Hills and Wyoming.* Aberdeen, SD: North Plains Press, 1984.

Gorzalka, Ann. *Wyoming's Territorial Sheriffs.* Glendo, WY: High Plains Press, 1998.

Holben, Richard. "Pickling Outlaws was a Form of Lynch Law Vengeance." *Frontier West,* December 1974, p. 22.

Mason, John. "Hanging of Big Nose George." *Real West,* January 1960, p. 17.

McClintock, John S. *Pioneer Days in the Black Hills.* Norman: University of Oklahoma Press, 1939.

Patterson, Richard. *The Train Robbery Era*. Boulder, CO: Pruett Publishing Company, 1991.

Spring, Agnes W. *The Cheyenne and Black Hills Stage and Express Routes*. Lincoln: University of Nebraska Press, 1948.

Wolfe, George D. "Curtains for Big Nose George." *True West*, April 1961, p. 18.

Henry Mosier and His Dog Tip: On a Crime Spree

Cheyenne (WY) Daily Leader: September 13–16, 1883; September 18–19, 1883.

George Cooke: He Had His Man for Thanksgiving

Albany County Criminal Court. Case file #181.

Beery, Gladys B. "He Died Game." *Real West*, Yearbook, Fall 1984, p. 31.

Brown, Larry K. *You Are Respectfully Invited to Attend My Execution*. Glendo, WY: High Plains Press, 1997.

Cheyenne (WY) Daily Leader: December 1, 1883; December 8–9, 1883; December 6, 1884; December 12–13, 1884.

Frye, Elnora L. *Atlas of Wyoming Outlaws at the Territorial Penitentiary*. Cheyenne: Wyoming Territorial Prison Corporation, 1990.

Laramie (WY) Weekly Sentinel: December 1, 1883.

Benjamin F. "Big Ben" Carter: The Badman from Bitter Creek

Brown, Larry K. *You Are Respectfully Invited to Attend My Execution.* Glendo, WY: High Plains Press, 1997.

Carbon County Criminal Court. Case file #180.

Cheyenne (WY) Daily Leader: October 26–28, 1888.

Frye, Elnora L. *Atlas of Wyoming Outlaws at the Territorial Penitentiary.* Cheyenne: Wyoming Territorial Prison Corporation, 1990.

The WSGA Lynching at Spring Creek Gulch

Anderson, Pete. "The Hanging of Cattle Kate." *True Western Adventures,* December 1960, p. 28.

Beachy, E. B. Dykes. "The Saga of Cattle Kate." *Frontier Times,* March 1964, p. 22.

Bommersbach, Jana. "So-called Cattle Kate Rises from Rubbish." *True West,* July 2005, p. 50.

Boucher, Leonard H. "The Wyoming Invaders." *Great West,* September 1969, p. 16.

Cheyenne (WY) Daily Leader: July 23, 1889.

Dickson, Ruth. "The Terrible Fate of Cattle Kate." *Big West,* August 1967, p. 11.

Hines, Lawrence. "Horror Lynching of the Petticoat Rustler." *Frontier West,* February 1973, p. 36.

Holding, Vera. "Cattle Kate, Queen of the Rustlers." *True Frontier,* September 1969, p. 42.

Hufsmith, George W., Jr. Ph.D. "Cattle Kate: A Total Lie." *True West,* May 2002, p. 45.

Keen, Cindy K. "Double Lynching in the Sweetwater Valley." *Wild West,* August 2002, p. 30.

Mumey, Nolie. "Behind a Woman's Skirt: The Saga of 'Cattle Kate.'" *Denver Westerners' Brand Book* no. 12, December 1950, p. 1.

Pons, A. C. "The Lynching of Cattle Kate." *The West,* March 1964, p. 34.

————. Rpt. *The West,* Annual 1971, p. 25.

Webb, Harry E. "With a Noose Around Her Neck." *Westerner,* May June 1972, p. 14.

George A. Black: A "Black Day" for Ol' Tanglefoot

Albany County Criminal Court. Case file #464.

Brown, Larry K. "Fingered by the Fire." *NOLA Quarterly;* October–December 1995, p. 29.

————. *You Are Respectfully Invited to Attend My Execution.* Glendo, WY: High Plains Press, 1997.

Cheyenne (WY) Daily Leader: February 26–27, 1890.

Frye, Elnora L. *Atlas of Wyoming Outlaws at the Territorial Penitentiary.* Cheyenne: Wyoming Territorial Prison Corporation, 1990.

Wyoming Territorial Supreme Court. Docket 2–76.

The Johnson County War

Anderson, Bryce W. "One Against An Army." *True West,* December 1956, p. 22.

Cheyenne (WY) Daily Leader: April 9–11, 1892; April 13–17, 1892; April 19, 1892.

Christy, Mort. "King of the Rustlers." *Real West,* August 1958, p. 16.

Hartley, William. "One Against Fifty-three." *True Western Adventures,* Summer 1958, p. 12.

Hutchins, John M. "The Good the Bad and the Ugly of Frank M. Canton, Alias Joe Horner." *The WOLA Journal,* no. 1, Spring 1994, p. 26.

Kelly, Bill. "The Death of Nate Champion and Nick Ray." *Real West,* September 1979, p. 24.

O'Neal, Bill. "100 Years Ago In The West." *Old West,* "Western Logbook" column, Summer 1993, p. 12.

Rickards, Colin. "Nate Champion Tells About the Wyoming Range War." *Real West,* March 1970, p. 58.

Vail, Jason. "Hired Assassins Dreaded." *Wild West,* June 1988, p. 20.

Wiltsey, Norman B. "The Saga of Nate Champion." Part I, *Real West,* April 1968, p. 22; Part II, Real West, May 1968, p. 48.

Winski, Norman. "Diary of a Cowboy About to Die." *Pioneer West,* November 1967, p. 42.

Butch Cassidy and the Sundance Kid: Those Elusive "Wild Bunch" Boys

Baker, Pearl. Utah 1890–1910, *The Wild Bunch at Robbers' Roost*. New York: Ballantine Books, 1965.

Buck, Daniel and Anne Meadows. "Butch & Sundance: Still Dead?" *NOLA Quarterly;* April–June 2006, p. 40.

Dullenty, Jim. "Wagner Train Robbery." *Old West*, Spring 1982, p. 40.

Ernst, Donna B. "Robbery Along the Great Northern." *True West*, June 1998, p. 46.

————. "The Wilcox Train Robbery." *Wild West*, June 1999, p. 34.

Horan, James D. *The Wild Bunch*. New York: Signet Books, 1958.

New York Times: July 3, 1901; July 6, 1901; July 8, 1901; October 16, 1901.

Overstreet, Charles. "A Train Robbery Turned Bad." *Old West*, Winter 1998, p. 49.

St. Louis Globe Democrat: November 29, 1892.

John "Badeye" Santamarazzo: The Weston County Poisoner

Frye, Elnora L. *Atlas of Wyoming Outlaws at the Territorial Penitentiary*. Cheyenne: Wyoming Territorial Prison Corporation, 1990.

Newcastle (WY) Democrat: August 15, 1895; April 23, 1896.

Stevens, Serita D., and Anne Klarner. *Deadly Doses, a writer's guide to poisons*. Cincinnati: Writer's Digest Books, 1990.

Weston County Court. Case file A-121.

Charles F. Woodard: The Murderer of Sheriff Ricker

Brown, Larry K. "A Bad Thing Happened One Good Friday." *True West*, April 2001, p. 42.

Cheyenne (WY) Daily Leader: March 28, 1902; March 29, 1902.

Natrona County (WY) Tribune: April 3, 1902.

Whipple, Dan. "To Die on Good Friday." *Wild West*, October 1996, p. 36.

Tom Horn: The Cattle Detective

Brown, Larry K. *You Are Respectfully Invited to Attend My Execution.* Glendo, WY: High Plains Press, 1997.

Browning, Dwain. "Tom Horn." *Great West*, October 1968, p. 18.

Carlson, Chip. "Tom Horn on Trial." *Wild West*, October 2001, p. 32.

Carson, John. "Tom Horn—was a hero or villain hanged?" *True West*, November–December 1960, p. 26.

Engebretson, Doug. *Empty Saddles, Forgotten Names; Outlaws of the Black Hills and Wyoming.* Aberdeen, SD: North Plains Press, 1984.

Koller, Joe. "Tom Horn: Man of Mystery." *Real West*, March 1971, p. 38.

McClintock, John S. *Pioneer Days in the Black Hills.* Norman: University of Oklahoma Press, 1939.

Repp, Ed E. "The Mystery of Tom Horn." *The West*, November 1968, p. 30.

About the Author

R. Michael Wilson has been researching the Old West for fifteen years, following a quarter century as a law enforcement officer. His particular interest is crime, and his writing philosophy is "the truth, the whole truth, and nothing but the truth."

Wilson served as a consultant for an episode of The History Channel's *Wild West Tech* and is an active member of the Wild West History Association (WWHA) and Western Writers of America (WWA).

Crime and punishment in America's early West is Wilson's area of interest and expertise. He is the author of *Great Stagecoach Robberies of the Old West*, *Great Train Robberies of the Old West*, *Frontier Justice in the Wild West*, *Tragic Jack: The True Story of Arizona Pioneer John William Swilling*, and *Massacre at Wickenburg*. He lives in Las Vegas, Nevada, with his wife Ursula.